MW01640991

Healing for the Other Woman

Vonnie White

Copyright©: 2022

All Rights Reserved

ISBN: 979-8-81-906485-6

Dedication

Healing for the Other Woman is dedicated to my sisters, my nieces, my cousins, my sister-friends, my coaches, my aunts, my daughters, my granddaughters, every woman, and ... my mother. When Jesus healed the woman with the issue of blood, it wasn't just for her, it was for ... The Other Woman ...

The title or label "Other Woman" is not given to a female based on the position a man places her in his life but rather the priority she allows herself to be in her own life.

Acknowledgements

LORD JESUS, I first and foremost give all praise and honor unto You for allowing me this opportunity. Your Word says in James 1:2, "Count it all joy, my brothers, when you meet trails of various kinds." And, Father, this journey has not been easy, but it has been worth it. I thank You for Your immeasurable love toward me. If I had a thousand tongues, I could never thank You enough. I pray this book will be a weapon of mass destruction against every weapon that has been formed to hinder and delay Your will on this earth.

To my Sweetie Pea. One of the most precious gifts GOD has bestowed upon me, King Jeremiah. No words can ever express the gratitude and honor I feel with each passing moment of being your mother. I thank GOD for choosing me to be the earthly vessel that birthed you. Your presence in this world is truly a gift I will never take for granted. I pray as you encounter life's events, you will forever remember what your name means: Jeremiah "appointed by GOD". No matter what anyone says, your focus will forever be on what GOD says about you.

Love Mommy

About the Author

Vonnie White, a vessel poured out for the Kingdom of GOD on this earth. She is anointed and appointed for such a time as this. She has been called and equipped to go unto the earth to teach the Word of GOD to those who have been chosen by GOD to break generational cures and further heaven's purpose on earth while making hell mad. To help others to differentiate between a "good" idea and a "GOD" idea. Between the Word and the World.

Vonnie owns and operates a real estate boutique, UnityRealty, which specializes in *"helping you find your place".* Where real estate is not only about buying and selling homes, but it is a ministry of service.

Vonnie is the founder and executive director of a non-profit organization, An Angel's Touch Foundation, which was established to *"strengthen communities one family at a time"* by investing in the lives of individuals while providing them with the tools, skills, and assistance needed to impact, affect, and unite their community.

Vonnie also owns and operates Kingdom Economics - a financial literacy program designed to empower students to become financially free, in addition to other business adventures and accomplishments.

Preface

Michael Jackson's song says, "I'm starting with the man in the mirror. I'm asking him to change his ways...." This was my heart's sentiment as I scrolled through social media, seeing so many women posting quotes and pictures of a life that appears to be happy but was counterfeit.

Healing for the Other Woman is to be that mirror illuminating the blind spots in our lives that have created generational patterns and belief systems.

Healing for the Other Woman is not about an adulteress affair. It is a healing hand being extended to Challenge the way we Prioritize ourselves. One day my son saw a family picture in my home of my mother, 3 brothers and myself and he asked "who is the little girl in this picture". I chuckled because he couldn't recognize her because I had not yet embraced the little girl in the picture. As I didn't recognize her as being me, either. This book begins with someone knocking on the front door of my house. This someone was not the wife of the man I was with. No it was the little girl within me who I had not recognized in my life just as my son did not recognize her in the picture. Therefore the cover of the book is me looking into a broken mirror but as Healing manifested within me. The little girl was recognizable by ME on the back of the book, and like me as you allow Holy Spirit to reveal in order to heal the broken places within your thought patterns and belief systems, your little girl will become recognizable to you as well.

This book is how GOD helped me with the "I Can". How I began to think better and higher about me and it will be a helping hand to you helping to change your view of you also.

Contents

Chapter 1: Healing for the Other Woman

Healing is a process known by many but taken by few. It is like a blessing awaiting to be availed.

The breeze brushing against my face was cold; the cold that has the feeling of ice in the air. It was about noon, on a beautiful day and the sun was shining ever so brightly. I could feel the warmth upon the skin of my face as the hot water covered my hands. I was in the kitchen of my home located to the rear of the house.

All of the windows were closed yet I could hear the birds chirping clearly as if I was standing in the midst of a garden. I was thinking about how much I truly enjoyed living in the suburbs, and the tranquility I felt as I looked out of the window. It brought on a sensation of solitude and peace. Unlike living in the city with loud sirens and horns echoing all around due to the constant traffic flow; this was a stillness. This was calming.

As I continued to wash the dishes and enjoy my peace. I was taken aback by the sudden noise of what sounded like a knock or a tap, but couldn't determine where it was coming from. The sound was so faint that I thought I was just hearing things. I continued with the dishes but then I heard it again. Tap Tap. I paused to try and figure out exactly what the sound was, and where it could be coming from. It almost sounded as if it was coming from the front door of the house, but I have a doorbell so why wouldn't they ring the bell was the thought I was having at that moment. Tap Tap. Now, I was looking over my shoulder as I simultaneously turned the running water off. I grabbed a paper towel and began walking in the direction of the front door. I walked past the TV that was on but muted and turned it off using the remote control wanting to make sure this sound wasn't coming from the TV. Continuing to the front door, I began pondering over this sound as it wasn't a constant knock or tap.

As I approached the door, I stood on the tip of my toes and looked through the peep hole. Nothing. I didn't see anyone, yet I now had this indescribable feeling. A feeling that someone could see me, but I couldn't see them. This feeling sent a chill up my spine. I turned from the door and as I took about three steps, I heard Bang Bang Bang. It startled me. I froze. I quickly turned around and heard Bang Bang Bang Bang — again. I thought, "Who could this be banging on my door as if they lived here?" The banging grew intense. I called out and asked, "Who is it?" No reply but the banging continued. I now had more force behind my question as I asked again, "who is it?"

Then what came next startled me more than the banging. What I heard next changed the course of my life. There was a slight pause and then I heard a woman's voice. Almost sobbing as she said, "It's me." The voice was somewhat familiar to me which made me cautious yet curious.

So, I slowly put one foot in front of the other and continued forward, toward the front door while asking the voice, "Who is me?"

Surprisingly, the tone of her voice changed as she yelled over and over with authority, "It's me, open the door, right now!"

It was at that moment I recognized who the voice belonged to, and it brought on a fear within me that I never felt before. This was a day I feared would come. So, in that very moment, I was on the floor now, right where I was standing, in the middle of the foyer, and drew my knees up to my chest. I first forced it to be a dream, but the longer I stayed on the floor, the longer she continued to bang on my door and kept demanding. Knowing she wasn't going to go away; I got up from the floor, trembling, and slowly began turning what felt like the coldest doorknob I had ever touched. It drew quiet as I began to open the door to see the face of the woman standing on the other side of the door. And to my surprise, the woman standing in front of me looked just like me. As this woman was none other than me. This discovery would indeed be a fight with me for me, as the enemy was within me.

"And we know that in ALL things (the good, the bad, the ugly, the shame, the guilt) GOD works for the good of those who LOVE THE LORD, who have been called according to HIS Purpose for them . . ." Romans 8:28

"I trust in YOU Lord; do not let me be put to shame..." Psalm 25:2

Father (ABBA), I thank you for your healing process. For allowing my sisters and me to walk through this journey, not alone but alongside you. Thank you for helping us to discover our mindsets and patterns that have led us to this place, and for anointing us with a fresh perspective (way of seeing) to guide us to a place called healed. Now Holy Spirit, we submit to Your mandates. In Jesus Might Name. AMEN (so be it)!

Chapter 2: Patterns and Perceptions - How Do We Get from Here?

Many times, we find ourselves in various positions. It's like LORD please tell me how to get from here. But before we can understand where we are, we have to understand how we arrived at this place in time. What were the thoughts and patterns that led us to this place?

When we think of the label "The Other Woman", we might think about a side chick, mistress, hoe, promiscuity, or cheater. But I'm coming before you to challenge this limited way we see "the other woman". First, the other woman is a sister, a friend, a daughter, a mother, a girlfriend, a wife. She's a woman just like you and me. She's the woman sitting beside you in church, in the choir, she's the First Lady at your church, she's the one singing your favorite songs in the music videos.

Chances are she's that little girl within you who's been crying and acting out, but you can't hear her, for all you have going on. She's the dreams you put on the shelf and said I'll get back to you later. She's the part of you who has taken the backseat to all of the other positions and labels you hold such as wife, main chick, mother, daughter, CEO, president, honor roll student, pastor, or friend.

She is the part of us that we don't deal with in hopes our husbands, boyfriends, children, religions, or careers will tend to, and if they don't, then she's the woman you cover up in all of the designer labels, hoping she won't be discovered. Yet eventually she will be discovered and oftentimes, that neglected woman within us manifests herself in many ways. Usually reckless ways, in hopes that you will tend to her and give her the attention she needs. Until we stop and heal her, she will show up at unexpected times, and act out in unexpected ways. She will come forth whenever you are in a vulnerable place in your life. Yes, that's right, the woman will start to act like the little girl she neglected until that little girl is healed. She will become a constant nagging voice in your subconscious mind talking to you about what you need to do, not to get hurt, but not about how you need to heal, and this is the reason I was led to share my journey of healing with you.

So, Sis, it is my prayer that you will ask Holy Spirit to open your mind as you partake on this journey of healing the other woman within. For the Bible tells us in Hebrews 12:27, "The final removal and transformation of all that can be shaken, that is, of that which has been created in order that what cannot be shaken may remain and continue". When we are called by GOD to be His vessels on this earth, there will come a time when He is going to do a shaking in our lives. Therefore, whatever we have been hiding behind and yet choosing not to deal with, GOD will remove it so that the authentic healed version of us will spring forth.

All of us have a little girl within. The question we must ask Holy Spirit is, "Has my little girl within grown and matured to a healthy woman in all areas of my life?" Meaning when you look into the mirror, is the image that your life is reflecting into the world Healed, Whole, and Healthy, or are some areas of your life infecting your environment? Creating toxic patterns and relationships with people, money, or community. For me, this little girl would often show up in my intimate relationships and how I spent money. After I would get close to someone intimately, I would often self-sabotage the relationship to push the person always and create a false narrative in my mind of how I wasn't good enough for them to stay around. Then after the distance was created between the person and me, I would often spend money on things that I would later justify as items or repairs needed. The truth was, I spent the money fast, hoping it too would not be taken from me. These were some of the ways the little girl within me would show up in reckless ways in my life, and I'm sure as you continue to read this book and employ HOLY SPIRIT in your innermost being, you too will discover how your little girl has been showing up.

Sis, we were created to be world changers. To affect and reflect on earth that which is in heaven. We are supposed to be the answer to the statement GOD made when He looked at the first man Adam and said, "It is not good for man to be alone, I will make a helper suitable for him" (Genesis 2:18). That helper was a woman. A woman who was whole. Therefore, Sis, we were created by GOD to affect our environment, community, and family, not to infect them. Sis, I thought I was whole by acquiring all of the labels, titles, and things of this world but I wasn't, and this is what the person on the other side of that door came to show me. What I had neglected, rejected, and even hid about me to the world but more importantly to myself. So let's begin....

Chapter 3: Not the Beginning but Not the End

Ding. That was the sound of an alert on my cell phone. I was in the kitchen, making my son some lunch for the afternoon. Preparing to sit down and relax after I'd fed him, I heard another "ding". I moved away from the stove to retrieve my phone and see what the alert was. It was a notification from Facebook telling me I had a message in my inbox. As I was reading the notification, I was thinking to myself, "what's an inbox on Facebook."

At this time in my life, I was new to all of the social media platforms and would only log in to them to post what I called "an awakening thought", so having an inbox message was new to me. I quickly discovered how to access this message. Once I retrieved it, the message read, "Hey, old love of my life." I looked at this message and thought about who this was and who he was referring to. Clearly, I didn't recognize the profile picture, so I then went to the messenger's page and realized who the individual was. Someone I prayed to forget, and it was evident I had.

I laughed and put my phone back down, not giving the message or the messenger a second thought. However, it may have been several months later but it was clear that the messenger had not forgotten me. Several months later, I was in my home office, finishing up an assignment I had to turn in that evening for school. I was in college full-time while attending to my home. My son had just turned three years old; I was attending classes, both online and on-campus, working in my real estate profession, and operating as a stay-at-home wife and mom. My plate was full of duties and no pleasure, but I didn't know this. I thought life was just peachy. So, on this sunny afternoon, while my son was taking his nap and I was working in my office, I heard that sound again. Ding. I laughed to myself as I stopped typing on the computer to pick up my phone.

I need a distraction anyway, I thought to myself. I was hoping it was a funny text message from my husband. But no, it was a Facebook alert again. Telling me I had a message in my inbox. I opened the notification, and the message read "Hey." I looked at the message and laughed. Then I thought to myself, "Old love of my life." I was remembering his previous message. Yet, this time I thought, what's the harm in replying? I told myself, "You're not interested in him and you need a distraction from this assignment." I would later discover this reoccurring pattern of entertaining distractions.

I replied, "Hi." Ding. He quickly replied and we started messaging back and forth. I started feeling all giggly inside like when you're a kid and a boy wants to talk to you. We started reflecting on the years that went by and then he asked me to call him because he was driving. Now this made me pause. I said no. Again, I'm a married woman and I didn't need to be texting with him nor did I need to be talking to him on the phone. When I communicated this to him, he insisted and said it would be okay and that he only wanted to continue our conversation but not have a car accident doing it. I reluctantly agreed. During the phone conversation, we laughed, and it felt refreshing. We continued to discuss our families and the fact that we both were married. He said he was married but separated, but I later learned this was not the truth. However, knowing my truth, I summarized that because we were both married, I wouldn't take our conversations seriously. I thought we were just catching up and nothing more. Again, nothing more than a distraction from my schoolwork. However, I must admit I was also thinking about how good it felt to hear someone tell me how he had a crush on me and how he thought about me often. Many say flattery often goes a long way, and I found this to be especially true when I was running on empty on this particular day.

You see the things this man was saying to me were conversations my husband and I did not have anymore, and now this man was awakening something in me that scared me. I found myself enjoying this edgy feeling. It was a feeling like you're about to jump into the deep of the ocean. Heart racing, palms sweating, adrenaline rushing, beads of sweat on your forehead, yet something inside is curious to feel the rush. To feel and explore something you've never experienced before. I was curious to know more about what I was feeling but knew this conversation was inappropriate.

When we got off the phone, I thought, "okay, that was a one-time thing. You will not have any more of these conversations." I guess I was trying to convince myself of this because the caller did not have these same reservations.

It is said that "curiosity killed the cat." Well, Sis, a woman is also referred to as a cat (Just food for thought). Because this cat was already flat-lined. Later, as the day turned into evening, my mind would often reflect on our call and it was like some sneaky sexy energy came over me. I knew this wasn't right. I'm a happily married woman, I kept telling myself, and he's a married man. When I went to bed that night, I tossed and turned uncontrollably. Why was I thinking of him? Why was this weighing so heavily on my heart and mind? I prayed and prayed until eventually, I got out of bed and went to my prayer closet. While praying in the closet I was asking God, "Why?" Why did I have that conversation with that man? Why was I still thinking about him? I had been married for 14 years and never once did I have an inappropriate conversation nor had I played around.

So why had I entertained the conversation? As I continued to sit in my closet, I started to remember some things the caller had said. He told me it was my fault we were not together, how much he had loved me when we were kids, and that we were supposed to have had kids together. All these statements kept replaying in my mind, as I continued to sit in this closet. I felt guilty. Not guilt over the conversation but the statements he made left me feeling as though it was actually my fault. Then, out of what seemed like nowhere, I started to remember how the bible talks about the sign of the marriage covenant being the shedding of blood from the woman's broken hymen.

Suddenly, tears started to form in my eyes. Then, I saw a vision as clear as a movie playing on a screen before my eyes, of the caller who we will refer to as 'B' and I, having sex and afterward, me having blood in my underwear. Now the tears were no longer building in my eyes but flowing down my cheeks as I remembered he was my first. He was the boy I shared my sacred space with, and now HOLY SPIRIT was revealing a soul tie between the caller and myself, because of the blood that was shed. A blood covenant was cut between us when he entered into my sacred space when I was 12 years old and did not realize it until that moment. I now saw myself spinning in a whirlwind, as I continued to cry. I visioned myself trying to grab hold of something to stop me from falling into this dark hole, but I couldn't seem to get a grip on anything. I saw my past intruding upon my present, and that it would ultimately impact my future.

Was this something I planned or prepared for? No. Yet, this was happening. I was screaming and falling, but no one could hear my screams or stop my fall. Not even me. This was the beginning of a process of learning and healing a part of me I had forgotten existed. You see I was at a place of busy, and busy can look very rewarding. Nice house (check), luxury cars (check), husband (check), child (check check check), businesses (check), income (check). I was so busy checking the boxes of life that I was not participating "in" life. I was busy, but not productive. I was nourished, but not healthy. I was filled, but not fulfilled.

I was alive, but not living life. The twinkle in my eyes went out and I never even noticed it was gone. Let alone when it even happened, and now, with the answering of an inbox message, I was about to go on a rollercoaster ride that wouldn't let me off even when I cried or prayed. Nope, I had to stay the course this time. I had bought a ticket and sat down in the seat. Buckled my seatbelt, because this ride would take me places I didn't want to go, and would keep me longer than I wanted to stay. Yes, Sis, it would ultimately cost me more than I wanted to pay. I was now at the bottom of this rollercoaster and I could hear the car going up the tracks. Crank by crank. I could tell I wasn't at the beginning, as this ride started long ago, yet I wasn't at the end either.

Chapter 4: Hide and Seek

"Search me and know my heart, test me and know my anxious thoughts..." Psalms 139-23

I've had the question asked, "Why do you think the other woman needs to be healed? No, instead she needs to get her butt whipped for messing with someone else's man." Here's the truth, ladies. If you are in a relationship or have been in a relationship where you were cheated on or treated unfairly; whatever the reason you entered into this relationship is the reason why healing is needed regardless of the situation. She, the other woman, is just a blind spot in your mirror.

Do you know why a car has side mirrors? It's to reflect the images of items we cannot see while looking ahead. And even with these side mirrors, we often cannot see the objects that are the closest to us. Therefore, we must make some adjustments to see the objects that are in our blind spots, and this is the process we are going to walk through together. The caller came along at that point in my life, to help me to discover myself.

To see parts of me I had neglected and allowed others to neglect as well. It is my hope and prayer that as I share my process of healing the other woman, you will discover yours as well. Sis, believe me, there is something within these pages for you too. You may not have had the same life experiences as me, but life has had experiences with you, your mother, and even your great grandmother, that have had an impact on your life. If you have ever asked yourself, "Why did I do that?" or "Why does this keep happening to me?" If you have ever set back and had a look at your relationship with money or food, and asked yourself, "Why am I eating this?" "Why haven't I lost weight?" "Why don't I have more money saved?" or even "Why am I still single and she is married?" Sis, the answer to these "why's" are in your mirror. However, the mirror will only reveal the answer to the why by asking questions.

But the Lord God called to the man "Where are you?" (Genesis 3:9)

"Who told you that you were naked?" The Lord God asked. (Genesis 3:11)

Then the Lord said to Cain "Why are you angry?" (Genesis 4:6)

When GOD revealed hidden truths to man, HE would often show them as a question. These questions were to help guide man into a truth that was within and was often not a *yes or no* answer. But to discover the answer, the man would have to search his heart to uncover the truth. As we continue on this journey of "healing for the other woman", we too will be asked questions that will require us to search our hearts for the truth no matter the cost. Sometimes, these truths may interrupt unhealthy thought patterns and belief systems. So, when we lose weight, it won't find us again. So, when we let go of the toxic relationships, we won't allow ourselves to re-enter new relationships with different names, only to reflect and produce the same toxic fruits. No, let's acknowledge the space and place we are in and allow Holy Spirit to do the work with us and through us, so we can discover the true version of Heaven's intent when it created us. Let’s allow our perspectives and perceptions of us to be healed from old patterns of thinking and behaving.

Pastor Joel Osteen once told a story during his sermon, about a family who would cut the butt of the ham off before cooking it. He said, when one member of the family was asked why it was done, she replied, “My grandmother did it, so we all did it.” When the grandmother was finally asked why she did it, she stated that her pan at the time was too small and the ham would not fit. So, she cut the butt off the ham so it could fit.

To discover the answer to our ‘whys’, we must be willing to ask and be asked about the hard and sometimes uncomfortable questions too. Why was I having a conversation when I was a married woman. He was a married man. I knew the difference between right and wrong. I wasn’t a thrill chaser. So, why? There were a lot of whys that went deeper than the conversations with this caller. As I allowed Holy Spirit to walk me along this journey, I discovered more questions than answers, and you will too, but don’t give up. Stay the course, for your healing is worth the cost.

I now understand that to be salt in someone’s life means to help them heal, and to be a believer or disciple for Christ JESUS would require healing. Therefore, I had to allow Jehovah-Rophe (the LORD who heals) to salt me. In biblical times when a baby was born, they would put salt on the baby to heal their wounds from birth. Like the salt used on the babies, GOD calls us to be salt to this world. Healing unto a broken and wounded (offended) world. This means we go through life events not only for ourselves but also for strengthening others. We don't encounter life events such as divorces, miscarriages, loss of a child, child custody battles, cancer, or loss of a loved one just for the sake of enduring it. No. In fact, I believe we are called to these life events not to break us but to strengthen the potency of our salt for the healing of others.

In Luke 22:32, JESUS tells Peter, "After you have come through this life event, go and help bring your brother through the same or similar life event" (me paraphrasing). Therefore, go and be healing salt to your brother who is struggling in the same area you were once struggling in. As now, you have a better understanding and empathy of how it feels to be afflicted in that area, I believe the other woman needs to be healed, not condemned or stoned.

Because I was her and she is me, I can now listen for understanding, not for judgment.

Chapter 5: Understanding Is the Truth You Stand Under

"Put First Things First..." Franklin Covey

Another misconception of being the other woman is limited to titles or labels, but I believe it is not about the title but about the position. You see whatever or whoever you value more than you, aside from GOD places you in the position of the "other woman." Which many times results in women becoming mistresses, side chicks, the neglected wife, or whatever the label we have decided to wear. Why? Because others cannot value you more than you value yourself. When your perspective of you is low, you will attract people and relationships who will have an equal or lesser perspective of you.

Let's say your title is wife, but your husband places the majority of his time, interest, or attention on making money, working, going out with the fellas, his car, his hobbies, or whatever it may be. Listen, it does not have to be another woman involved to make you the other woman. It just means that you are not prioritized or positioned above these other things in his life. Why? Because you have not first made the way you view yourself, worth a priority in your own eyes. Failing to do so will result in a part of you becoming "the other woman" in your marriage. The Bible says, that before we can deal with others, we have to first deal with ourselves. Matthew 7:5 says, "...First get rid of the log in your own eye;

then you will see enough to deal with the speck in your friend's eye."

This scripture is telling us to first change the way we see ourselves before we focus on the way someone else is seeing or prioritizing us. We often hear the saying, Location Location Location! But in our lives, Sis, it's about Priority, Priority, Priority. And, Sis, sometimes this neglected wife may become another man's mistress.... as I did but we'll get into that later. Yeah, I know right, me. Speaking in tongues, faith-filled, Spirit-walking, ordained me. Yup, as a title or our faith does not exempt us from trouble. In fact, it actually attracts trouble. Especially, if we are not examining ourselves honestly daily, and humbling ourselves before the Lord daily. Neglecting us usually means we are neglecting our "relationship with Holy Spirit". Which will allow pride to rise up, and we know pride comes before the fall.

As for me, this woman showed up on my doorstep and demanded to come in. She decided she would no longer play her role anymore, and she wanted me to know why.

Now, before we go any further, please let me say I am not making any excuses for cheating. Not by any means. What I am saying to every woman who has found herself in the position of being the other woman, no matter the circumstance, healing is available.

It is my hope that as I share my journey of healing, you find something that speaks to that neglected part within. I must say, this journey has not been easy, but it has been worth it because I get to talk to you. I had to come to a place of acceptance. Acceptance of me and everything I have been through. I had to come to an understanding of myself without judgment, and this is my prayer for you also. Healing is a process. One which we cannot do alone. It will require backup from the Holy Spirit. It will exercise your patience, test your faith, and reinforce your trust in JESUS. But Sis we can do it together, so let's get healed. As I share my process with you, it is my hope you see and understand how I arrived at the place of being the other woman and how you did also. We must first understand how we arrived at a destination, in order to move from that place. We must acknowledge the thought patterns and belief systems that led us to this place of self-neglect. We must understand that we were created by a perfect God, but we ourselves are not perfect.

Yet we are imperfectly perfected through the life events and decisions they came to teach us. In fact, it is my belief that it is these non-perfect life events and decisions that teach us the best lessons and add flavor to our salt. Therefore, as we continue to journey together seeking healing for the other woman, it is my prayer that you will be patient, loving, gentle, and understanding with yourself. Know that we are bound to make mistakes and there is no such creature in this world that could be taken as perfect. Therefore, it is important to accept and understand oneself and the mistakes attached to us, without any judgment and blaming. Only then with the knowledge of understanding of oneself will you be able to heal. As healing starts first from the place of self-discovery from the inside out.

I pray GOD will give you the knowledge of understanding without judgment, as you unfold these pages.

Chapter 6: The Pressing and the Process

"And let us not be weary in well doing: for in due season we shall reap, if we faint not." Galatians 6:9

Press means: To exert weight or force. To embrace, to urge on.

Process means: A natural phenomenon marked **by gradual changes,** that lead toward a particular result. (Also known as a course).

As stated in the previous chapter, in order to understand where we are, we must first understand the choices and decisions that led us here. I am going to show you how I arrived at the place of being the other woman, as I parallel life's journey and the wine-making process. Prior to the evening of the original phone call, I would often envision how I thought my life would turn out. God would often show me a vision or snippets of future events in my life. The problem with being shown a vision is, you do not know how or when that vision will come to pass, and that vision requires a process.

In God's word, we see many people receiving visions or promises. When they received the vision, promise, or prophesy, they didn't know they were entering the door of process. This means God will reveal a destination or an outcome to you, and then HE will send you to or drop you off at a school; called process. We see this with both, David and Joseph. God showed both of them a vision of their future and then took them through a process that led to the promise. It is during this time of the process that God shows us who we are in order for us to truly see who He is. The process is required to prepare us for what God has prepared for us. The process develops and matures the way we perceive information. The process comes to heal the underdeveloped mindsets. As we live forward, we understand backward. We have to go through the processes of life, to truly understand how to live.

I am going to walk you through a process of making wine referred to as "winepress", and parallel this process with our life process.

Let's first consider how wine is made, and the key component in wine: the grape. Before a grape takes its true form, it is first a seed, and as we know, a seed unplanted is just a seed. In Luke 8:11, JESUS reveals to us that the seed in our life is the Word of God, and just like the grape seed, it must be planted on good ground which is our heart, Luke 8:8. But as we know, our ground is not always a good ground. As our ground is often contaminated with many of life's events, creating hard not easily yielding areas within our ground, and because our ground is still hard and rocky with life's issues, it needs to be cultivated by God, who is the gardener, John 15:1.

Therefore, when we surrender our hearts to God, HE is now our groundkeeper, and HE will start to work our ground, which is known as "a process". I say a process because there will be many processes. Therefore, it is important to remember that when we give our lives to God, and we start on our course, it's similar to when we were kids and we started school. We first went to pre-k, then to kindergarten. As children of God, we are first babes in Christ drinking milk, and just as there was a process to move from one grade to another, so will we go from one level of understanding to another, knowing that as one process finishes, another one is beginning. We will forever be students at this thing called life, and as we walk with God, the process changes from level to level or glory to glory. It will be important to our growth and development that we stick with the process.

That even when our knees are weary and our back is aching, we do not break down in the process, and forfeit the promise, because just like in grade school, you will have to stay there until you pass. An example of this can be seen in the wilderness with the Israelites. When God brought them out of Egypt which He referred to as bondage, many of the Israelites fainted during the process and never made it to the promise, and the process that was to take seven days lasted 40 years.

Can you relate to this? I can. There have been many things in my life I look back at and say, "If only I had stayed the course and not given up I would have accomplished this by now." Like wanting to lose weight. I have had a goal to lose weight for several years. I went to many doctors and received different protocols that actually worked. These plans usually required me to eat healthier and to exercise more often. I would leave these doctors motivated and focused. I would work with the plan and get rewarding results.

However, somewhere along the process, I would stop doing what I knew worked. I would stop the process and forfeit the promise of weight loss. I did this for years. Every year, I would have the same goal, yet something inside of me would not allow me to finish. I would look back over the year and say, "If you would have stayed focused and consistent, you would have accomplished this goal already," and you know what, that fact was true. If I would have stayed the course, I would have accomplished this goal. However, when I did decide to allow Holy Spirit into this process to coach and guide me through; I discovered amazing things about myself. Yes, I lost the weight that was weighing my body down, but I also lost the weight that was weighing my mind down.

Sis, will this process be easy? No, but it will be worth it. Just like with the process the grape must endure, so must we endure the process set before us to become the masterpiece God created us to be. We, like the grape, will endure some pressing, some sifting, some waiting. I don't know how long this process of healing will take you, but it is my hope and prayer that when you feel like giving up you won't. That you will employ Holy Spirit to shine God's light on that mindset that is trying to prevent the higher version of yourself from manifesting the promise. I pray you will seek wise counsel and a relationship with Holy Spirit, as you continue on the process of healing the other woman, knowing that I am your sister on this journey with you. Holding your hand in those dark places, praying for your continued endurance.

Phase One...

Chapter 7: Seeding

"The seed falling on rocky ground refers to someone who hears the word and at once receives it with joy. But since they have no root, they last only a short time. When trouble or persecution comes because of the word, they quickly fall away." Matthew 13:20-21

Phase one in the wine-making process is called "seeding". Remember, we have to develop fruit before we can harvest it for the wine and in this case, we need to harvest grapes. Let's take a look at the seeding process. In Luke 1:28-38, we see the angel of God imparting Mary with a vision, and her receiving the word and planting it in her heart. Luke 1:38.

I like to say, "I was birthed for such a time as this," to break a cycle that has repeated itself through generations within my family. In Hebrew, the number four represents, "Open doors or new beginnings," and let's just say my birthdate is comprised of all fours. So, I guess I didn't choose this path, it chose me, and here is my seeding process.

Mommy's Baby

When my father met my mother, she was a beautiful attractive married woman, but she didn't know it. You see my mother was the oldest daughter of sixteen kids, twelve of which were boys. Growing up, my mother says her brothers would tease her and call her ugly. They told her she had a big nose ("I like my man with Jackson Five nostrils" ... quote from Beyoncé). When she was attending grade school, many girls would tease her and pull her hair. She did not have the latest fashions and would often feel left out. She never felt pretty, smart, or good enough. She lacked confidence in herself.

My mother had her first child when she was 17, and my grandmother sent her to live in a girl's home, where she would later give birth to my oldest sister. This separation and isolation planted a seed of abandonment within my mother, and as life went on, many men would water this seed. Resulting in her becoming a single mother of three, early in her 20s. When she did decide to marry, it was to a man she didn't love and this marriage produced her fourth child. I was her sixth child. Having seeds of abandonment planted within her would also cause the ground of her heart and womb to become contaminated. Therefore, when she incubated me within the ground of her womb, I along with my siblings, received improper nourishment. I received the contaminants of abandonment, and instead of me properly developing emotionally, I became emotionally malnourished.

Daddy's Maybe

I don't know much about my father's childhood. Truth is, I don't even know how many siblings he has. But what I do know is the story he told me one day, when he was in the hospital after having a mild stroke. He recalled the only time or the last time he saw his dad. He says, he was in his mother's arms and his dad was in a hospital bed, and this was his only memory of his dad.

After graduating high school in the south. He received a football scholarship to Howard University, where he graduated as a civil engineer. After graduating, he took a job in his field in the city, when his high school girlfriend who was still down south, informed him she was pregnant. He stated that being from the south and a Christian, he did what he thought was right and married her, and he moved her to be with him. Now, this doesn't mean he didn't love her. It just means he did what many had done. Turn a good idea into a God idea. After they wed, he attended a prenatal appointment with his wife and was told by her physician that she was never pregnant. This planted a seed of betrayal and fear within my dad, and like my mom, with time and life experiences these seeds continued to grow and develop.

Later as life has it, my mom and dad now live in the same neighborhood. Both of them are married to other people, but neither one is fulfilled. They were both searching for something. After meeting through my mother's then-husband, she and my father began a relationship neither divorced but still married. Prior to meeting my dad, my mom had her tubes tied as she now had four children, but my dad didn't have any children yet. He asked my mom to untie her tubes, and she did, resulting in the birth of my brother and me.

As my mother later told me the story of her and my dad, she stated that when my brother was born, my dad felt my brother was the "seed of his seed". However, when I was born, my dad felt the need to get a DNA test for me. My mother stated he said, "She is too light and pretty to be my daughter," as he looked upon me after birth. So, at birth where my dad was supposed to command and speak a blessing over my life, he unknowingly cursed me. You see he said, "She's too pretty to be my daughter."

So instead of me feeling and believing I was ever pretty growing up, I felt the opposite. I felt unattractive, untrusting (betrayal), and abandoned. I actually felt like my parents stole me from the hospital, switched me at birth, and that I belonged to someone else. His statement "to be my daughter" planted seeds of rejection in me. A feeling of never belonging. My mom often reminded me that when she was pregnant with me, she considered aborting me due to the environment surrounding her relationship with my dad.

Hearing my mother recite these events over and over throughout my life, led me to develop a fear of someone close to me leaving me. That once I loved someone, they would not want me for me so the seeds of abandonment, rejection, distrust continued to develop and grow in the ground of my heart. Leading me to self-abandon and self-rejection. I became fearful of being vulnerable with others. Fearing they would not like me for me and that I would not measure up to who they thought I was. Just like the feeling I had from the statements my parents made toward me.

My parents' volatile relationship led to them separating when I was about four years old. Resulting in daddy no longer living in the home with us, which caused my brother and me to see him less and less. Many times, my brother and I would make several attempts to reach him, and sometimes he wouldn't even return our calls. He would often make empty promises. This empty space within me led to a longing and an expectation of disappointment. This was the beginning of the seeding process for me and during incubation, several seeds were planted within the ground of my heart and my soul. As with life experiences, many people would water these seeds causing them to grow into my adult life. Often it is said, "You can't really know where you are going until you know where you have been." (Maya Angelou) In other words, in order to know why you have arrived at a particular place, you have to first understand the road that was first taken to lead you there.

For me, I had to spend time with The One who first knew me. I would often pray and ask God to show me who I am before life placed its hands on me. This part of the process led me to ask questions, sit with the answers, and pray for the revelation of truth. I hope on your process of "Healing the Other Woman", you will reflect on your conception and the earthly vessels that united to create the priceless, one-of-a-kind masterpiece, called You. Yes, Sis, this is why I am here for you.

To extend a hand during the trying and difficult times of this healing process. It is my hope that you will make this book a part of the tools that will help you to plant and un-plant generational thoughts, beliefs, and patterns that may have been planted by your mother, father, or both. Knowing that these thoughts, beliefs, and patterns may not have originated with us, but they can end with us. Then, we can start to produce healthy healed thoughts, beliefs, and patterns for our children and those we come in contact with. During this stage of the process, it will be important to journalize your thoughts.

As you seek truth at this stage, the truth will be revealed. I found it easier to write down what was being revealed to me. Sometimes, this revelation will come while you're reading this book, driving, or lying in silence. Oftentimes, it may come in pieces, and journalizing gives you something to reflect on, to help make sense of the pieces. Again, I hope as you hold this book, you know that I am your Sister in the process with you holding your hand pointing to The Gardner who is holding you in His hand.

Nevertheless, it is important to look into the big picture and trust the process. I know you must have heard this phrase quite a lot of times, but just go through it once more, slowly. "Trust - the - process." Belief is always the first step toward achieving the goal. Until and unless you understand and put your trust in the process, it's impossible for you to move on and get to the vision you have in mind. Confusion never leads to a straight road, but only worsens it.

Remember, when asking the "why" questions, we are often led to other questions like "What was the ground I was incubated in?" What did mommy think life was like when she incubated me? The Bible says, "With all thy getting, get understanding" (Proverbs 4:7). Gaining an understanding of what seeds were planted in our ground will help to gain wisdom for healing. Also please remember we are asking Holy Spirit to reveal knowledge for understanding for us to heal not to judge our parents, our past, or ourselves.

Holy One of Israel, I humble myself before You thanking You for Your revelation knowledge with the understanding that has been bestowed upon my sister this day. I thank You for the peace it has brought with it to reside in her heart. We trust and rely solely on You. Thank You for the love that causes us to forget. Forget the pain, the shame, guilt, blame, fear, and anything else Holy Spirit has revealed. For Your Word says, "perfect love drives out fear." So, we thank You for this perfect love. In Jesus' Mighty Name, Amen.

Chapter 8: Way Forward

"Wait on the Lord; be of good courage, and He shall strengthen thine heart. Wait, I say on the Lord!" Psalm 27:14

Now that we have our seed and we have planted it in our heart (the ground). We now need some water. 1 Corinthians 3:6 says, "I have planted, Apollos watered; but God gave the increase." It is during this stage in the process many people will come along and water us and what they water us with will be dependent upon the motive or objective of the waterer. When Jesus was on the cross, He said, "I thirst," and instead of giving Him water, they gave Him vinegar John 19:28-29. Many people will come into our lives and water us with anything but the word of God. What God says about us.

I was six years old when I was hit by a car as I was crossing the street. Many people thought I would never walk the same as my pelvis was fractured. I was often told I would never be able to have children. It was during this time in my life I learned how to endure pain and how to use pain for love. Because of my age at the time of the accident, I did not have corrective surgery. Instead, I had to endure my pelvic bone constantly moving in and out of place which would have me in severe pain. As I mentioned previously, my dad was no longer living in the home with me so as the pain would come, I would hope and pray this would also bring him back to me. I would oftentimes dream of my dad coming to my rescue like a night and shining armor, but it didn't make him come around more. In fact, it's like the more I expressed pain the less I saw my dad resulting in rejection of self-expression. When I was experiencing pain my mother and siblings would often feel sorry for me and spend a little more time with me. Yet I would also overhear them telling others how much I could not have children, and this made me feel inadequate. So, I would often overcompensate to prove that I wasn't broken but yet worthy to be loved.

I was twelve years old when I met the caller who I will refer to as B. We lived in the same community and attended the same school. B would have been sixteen years old at the time. On serval occasions, I can recall him trying to talk to me and I would ignore him. The truth is I wasn't attracted to him. Back then I was attracted to more of an Al B. Sure! American singer-songwriter type of guy. The six feet tall, muscular build, light skin tone, and wavy hair. I chuckle because this was not the typical guy in my neighborhood, but as time went on and B's persistence I gave in or should I say fell in.

Many times, he and I would be on the playground kissing. I enjoyed kissing him. Funny I can still smell his breath and feel his lips. Don't get me wrong he did not have bad breath at all. His body had this unique masculine scent. It was like the right mix of rough and right. During this time, he would always send me home with hickey marks on me and, of course, smelling like him. I would have to hide these marks from my mom.

One day, she saw one on my neck, and instead of punishing me, she told me why these marks were not good for me. She informed me that a hickey was more than a love bite but was actually bruised blood. I would not allow him to do this to me anymore. Now let me paint a picture for you. I was one of those little girls who developed physically early. Breast and hips at the age of six. Menstrual cycle at the age of nine and major determination since birth. So, when my family and I moved to this community many of the neighborhood guys would want to get with me and I knew they really only wanted sex so I would avoid a lot of them. I reluctantly gave in to B.

One night, B and his friend came over to my friend's house where I'm staying. I remember us being on her bunk bed and allowing him into my sacred space as I put my virginity in his hands. I remember going to the bathroom afterward and I was bleeding. Not heavy but more like spotting. Early the next morning the four of us were in the hallway of the building talking and I remember my stomach hurting. I was nervous. What did I just do? Now he's about to act up... I told myself. He just kept smiling and his friend making jokes. I guess he already told them and now the jokes on me I said to no one but myself.

A short while after B and I continued to see each other and have sex he brought a bag of all this broken jewelry to me, and in it was a ring. I remember him wanting me to wear this broken ring that would hurt my finger. It would pinch my finger causing pain. Being young I wore it until the pain became embarrassing and I eventually removed it. As I reflect on that moment in time, I believe the pain from the ring was a sign or a clue to the pain that would later come back in my life. Pain is like those life alert buttons some seniors wear around their neck to alert the authorities they are in pain and need help. Pain is an indicator that something that we cannot see within us is having a problem, and the pain is trying to alert us of this problem. Later in life, this internal problem would reveal itself to me. One day during our relationship we must have made plans for me to come over to his house. When I arrived, the door opened slowly as two females walked out. These were girls I knew from the neighborhood. I looked over their shoulders and I saw him coming out of his room with boxers on with this grin on his face. Now I'm hurt and embarrassed, but I wouldn't let it show. I turned and left without a word.

That day I maintained my composure on the outside but on the inside, I was broken. That night I balled up in a corner in my mom's bed and cried. I prayed and asked God for several things. First, to never let me feel this way ever again. I never wanted to love or care for another man the way I loved and cared for B as doing so gave them the power to hurt me. Second, to block B out of my mind so I could never remember him again. I was asking God for emotional amnesia.

Lastly, I asked never to have children because I didn't want to birth a daughter to feel the pain I constantly felt since I was born. First, the rejection and abandonment I felt from my parent and now the betrayal, rejection, abandonment, and heartbreak I was feeling from B. I didn't want my children to experience this loveless world. I believe God answered my request. Whenever B would come around me, I didn't even notice him. I was cold as ice. He would make several attempts to tell me the girls were not at his apartment for him, but I was totally numb at this point. He didn't exist, what we shared didn't happen, and I told myself it didn't matter. To get over it and move on. As time and life went on, I moved on and he moved away. If he sent a message to me, it didn't even faze me. The feelings I had for him were gone. As if they never existed or so I thought. I didn't even relate him to the loss of my virginity. I blocked his very existence out. I buried this pain or should I say planted this pain. You see there is a difference between something being buried and something being planted. When something is buried, it means it's dead, but when something is planted, it is still alive. It may look dead or lifeless but with water and time, it will spring forth.

Whether good or bad. This pain was planted and with much watering from other guys and time, it revealed what was indeed within. Those words of me not being able to have children sprung forth as the fruit of inadequacy. I felt as though I didn't measure up to other girls and I carried those same thoughts into my adult life. That day when I saw B with those other girls it was like validation that I was not enough and that I was inadequate which kept me looking and comparing myself to others in the hope I would not be singled out as different but accepted and worthy in man's eyes of love.

Sis, this stage for me in the process of healing was difficult. I cried a lot as God reminded me of these events. Had many restless nights. I would often pray and ask God to show me who He created me to be before life placed its hands on me, and when praying this type of prayer, I had no idea the revelation that would come. I didn't like my reality of the truth and I felt rejected all over again. Until one day I read in God's Word that I was accepted. Ephesians 1:6 told me I was "accepted into the Beloved". I understood then that I was God's child and He did not reject me but He accepted me just as I am. In spite of life choices, I am accepted. This brought peace to me. When we are being watered, we must learn the difference between what God said and what man said no matter who that man or woman was in our life. We have to also be careful not to get into agreement with what man says but only with what God says.

I believed that because I was injured in the car accident, I was damaged goods. I believed what I often heard and this belief created an agreement with what was being said. I would hear what man said and repeat it versus repeating what God was saying about me. God was saying "you are the head and not the tail, you will only be above and not beneath" Deuteronomy 28:13. However, in order to know what God was saying about me, I had to get the water of God's Word down in my heart (ground) and allow His Word to take root.

2 Timothy 2:15: "Study to show thyself approved unto God, a workman that need not be ashamed...." When we are being

watered by the Word of God, we will come to a place of knowing God for ourselves. This place will also require us to believe His Word. Luke 1:45. Therefore when waterers (people) try to pour in that which is not of God the Word will separate God's Word from man's opinions. Heb 4:12. But remember we can't skip the planting process or there will be nothing there to discern the thoughts and intents of the heart. Reflecting back to my seeding process when I really started reading the Word of God for myself God brought some wonderful women into my life to help me understand what I was going through. To show me and not just tell me I was not alone. To remind me of what God says about me and Sis this is why I am here for you. To be a hand along the way to your healing. To be that coach in the corner of your mind reminding you of the greatness God planted in you before you were placed in your mother's womb before life touched you. That no matter what you did or didn't get as a child. Who did or didn't say "I love you," and no matter who did or didn't stay? Sis, you are wonderfully and marvelously made and you are Purposed. Healing is yours for the taking and a part of your process.

Chapter 9: Grounding

"From that time on JESUS began to explain to his disciples that he must go to Jerusalem and suffer many things at the hands of the elders, the chief priest and teachers of the law, and that he must be killed and on the third day be raised to life." Matthew 16:21

Now there have been many examples of the process in the Bible, but the ultimate example for us was JESUS. Many times, we just reflect on the cross but we forget that He had to go through a process that led to the cross. JESUS was the only one that went through a process to be a living example of God's love for us. Meaning He went through the process not for Himself but for us. I also believe God allowed me to go through this process not just for me but Sis, for you also. To show you that healing is possible, but it will require a process. That during this process of planting and watering we have to seek God for understanding.

God is asking, not demanding, to reveal Himself to you as The Gardener who wants to tend to the ground of your heart. Here's what He says, "Let Me expose and reveal the contaminated thought patterns and belief systems that have been planted in your ground so I can heal your heart. For I will give you the desires of your heart, but first let's heal your heart, so these desires match the desires I have already predestined for you. As these things are already yours. "For as he thinketh in his heart, so is he." Proverbs 23:7.

There are some thought patterns and belief systems that you have allowed to take root in the ground of your heart by meditating on negative thoughts such as, I'm not good enough, I'm not worthy, my dad wasn't there for me, I'm flawed, I'm not pretty, or even I'm a sinner. All of these thought patterns came from negative belief systems and now I need a software reset of these systems. For I want to reset the thought patterns and belief systems that have cluttered your mind long enough causing these negative patterns to shape your life. I want to clear out the things you have said about you that do not mirror the thoughts I have for you. Until the things you say about you match and mirror the thoughts and things I say about you".

Allowing Holy Spirit to water us with the Word of God. Allowing it to penetrate the ground of our hearts to counteract the side effects of the words, actions, and events that have been planted in our life by people's opinions. Yes, these things happened, and more life experiences will develop. However, when we allow The Healer, The Gardner, Holy Spirit to come in and heal our heart, eyes, and mind we can gain a clearer perspective of what took place. Yes, the event happened. Yes, there were words spoken. But yes, God accepts you just as you are even though those things happened, and yes, He loves you. Like myself, I hope you will spend time allowing the process to unfold knowing healing is on the other side.

Knowing that I am your Sister in the process with you holding your hand pointing to The Gardener who is holding you in His hand. You will know when healing has taken place at this stage because you would have matured to a place where you no longer ask the question "why". Then we will know The Healer has healed this part within.

"He will have no fear of bad news; his heart is steadfast Trusting in The LORD" ...Psalm 112:7

Chapter 10: Running on Empty

"I would have fainted, unless I had believed that I would see the goodness of the Lord in the land of the living." Psalm 27:13

After the breakdown over B, I believed that any boy who was interested in me was only interested in my body. I was an early developer as a child and therefore many of the guys who were interested in me were much older, and since it did not work out with B I now had no interest in most boys my age. I thought the older guys would treat me better than B did, but I soon discovered this was not the case either. I discovered that sex was the only thing they wanted from me or at least that is how I felt. I placed my worth and value in my sexuality.

I had been pursued for sex since I was nine years old, but I never gave in to the attempts. So, when B pursued me, I was hoping for something real. I thought if I gave myself to him and allowed him into my sacred space that he would actually see me and choose me as his girl. That his motive would be pure. That he actually wanted me for more than sex. I mean come on he pursued me for quite some time and when I agreed to be his girlfriend, he did things that made me believe what he was telling me was true.

One particular day, he gave me a bag of jewelry. I clearly thought this meant he liked me, right? No, because soon after he accomplished his mission of entering my sacred space, he was on to the next girl, and this became a pattern in my life. I realized then that money, gifts, material things, or even nice words spoken with ill intent do not equal reciprocity. Just because someone is telling you what they think you need to hear and spending money on you does not mean they love you or are committed and loyal to you. It doesn't even mean they truly care for you. But that all of these exchanges do come with a cost. Remember I said earlier that these misguided choices would cost me more than I wanted to pay. Well, allowing guys to enter into my sacred space who were not preauthorized by heaven cost me greatly. Therefore, many times, when I would find myself in this pattern of thinking a guy was really interested in me, I would just give in to him and allow him into my sacred space to avoid rejection if I objected to his pursuits. Only to discover it was the same pattern or guy just with a different name. This pattern of misguided behavior led to me tucking my heart away and moving on. Why did I move on without processing my true feelings and emotions? It was for my survival. I have come to learn that if I had stopped and focused on what I was truly experiencing and what it was costing me, I may not have survived.

"For what shall it profit a man, if he shall gain the whole world, and lose his own soul(heart)? Mark 8:36 ...

Answer. There is no profit

Profit is what you have left over at the end of a transaction. So when the scripture says there is no profit, what it is stating is that after the transaction was finished there was nothing left, e.g., 0 × 10 = 0.

You may have started out with 10 but remember that empty glass. If you keep pouring out into empty glasses, you will be left empty. Why? Because what you are pouring into is not reciprocating by pouring back into you. Relationships are created to be a place of exchange sometimes referred to as give and take. However, if you are constantly pouring out and that person is not pouring back into you, your glass will soon be empty. Many times, when a person has a giver's heart. They will pour out to others without the expectations of receiving which can have a downside, because they may not know they are depleted or drained until there is nothing else left. The person on the receiving end who doesn't pour back into the giver will often devalue the gift given because it didn't cost them anything. This results from the receiver not giving anything back in exchange for the gift that was given.

It is important for us to learn that the gift given did not cost the receiver anything. The gift still came at a cost to the giver. If I buy you, Sis, a gift, the gift will cost me. I had to buy it with money or talent, and time, but when I give it to you it will be no cost to you. However, it cost me the giver something. Many times, when we are on the receiving end, we never look at what it cost the giver. In my case with B and all that came after him, it was costing me my self-worth, my integrity, and my time with each transaction.

I have learned that I can gain back my self-worth and my integrity, but I can never regain or be repaid for the time exchanged for these misguided choices. As time is one of the greatest prices we will pay for misguided choices. We all are on this earth for a finite time. We have a specific number of days we will be on this earth, and we need to spend this time wisely. Therefore, it is imperative Sis; we receive healing for the other woman. God is the Healer and He has given us this day the choice between life and death.... choose life (Deuteronomy 30:19). When we choose life, we choose to allow the Healer to heal us. To refill our empty glass. To place us in healthy relationships that will be an exchange, and to be aware of the choices we are making moving forward knowing the cost associated with these choices.

Chapter 11: Prices We Pay

"Or what shall a man give in exchange for his soul?" ***Mark 8:37***

Another price we will pay for misguided choices is our soul. I had been exchanging my soul for love and acceptance from a man since birth. That first man being my dad my first earthly love of a man and the next being B. Therefore, my glass did not start empty when I met B it became empty over time. In fact, when I met B my glass was already less than full. The absence of my dad physically, and mentally from my mom had already caused drainage from my glass. However, the encounter with B helped my already unfilled glass to continue to be drained, and for the next two years, I became promiscuous.

The relationship with B in my youth was like the first high someone feels after doing drugs. It's a high you can't quite explain but you want that feeling again. B made me feel pretty and special like I was being seen. In my house growing up, I never felt like I was actually being seen. Also, when B hugged me I felt safe. Not that B was protecting me from anyone hurting me, but it was a safe feeling a little girl looks for in her father's arms, and I felt this in B's arms.

When I was with B, I often felt a feeling of being all warm inside. This was a feeling like drinking hot cocoa on a cold snowy night type of warm, and I wanted to feel that warmth continuously. The problem with this type of feeling is that it is not continuous. Therefore, like a drug I kept getting high searching for that initial feeling. I kept searching for that high with every guy that would come along. Hoping the next one would give me that same warm hot cocoa feeling or better. But it never happened. That I would feel safe in their embrace, but that never happened either. They say in Narcotics Anonymous that "one is too many and a thousand is never enough." Meaning the first high is one too many and a thousand highs will never be enough. We often keep searching for that first euphoric feeling hoping and praying the next relationship will fulfill what's missing but it doesn't. Instead with each relationship and with each sexual encounter the already empty glass begins to break.

Therefore, by the time I was 14 and met the guy who at 20 would become my husband, I was beyond empty and in need of healing for my weary soul. I had exchanged it for love and only received lust. I learned that if I truly liked a guy, he had the potential to hurt me. So, I began to refer to the relationships I encountered as safe. Not really liking anyone. Therefore, when my then-husband came along and offered what appeared to be a little different, I took it. Why? Because I was at zero. My glass was empty. I had poured out all that was within me at that time, and I had nothing left to fight with. I couldn't run any longer and was too dehydrated to make the best choices for myself. So, I chose what was choosing me.... survival at the cost of my soul.

The Word tells us, "For God so loves the world that He gave His only son," and Jesus gave up His life in order for us to have everlasting life. He gave His life so we can have eternal life with Christ JESUS. We now have salvation. We can now pray to the Father through Christ JESUS, and this gift is free to us, but it was not free to JESUS. No, it cost Him something. HE was accused, rejected, beaten, and crucified for our salvation. So, when we are making life decisions, we must assess the cost. Many times, we see someone with a nice luxury car or house and think "I want that," but we never stop to ask how much it cost or what is it costing them. For the cost is not always something we can quantify. No. There is no amount of money I could associate with losing my soul. Every time I settled for less to prove I was worthy of love it was costing me a piece of my soul.

I had been operating from a deficiency from the day I was placed in my mother's womb and she contemplated aborting me, and when my father first saw me and thought I was not his child. These events were out of my control but were glass emptying moments. These were moments that set the atmosphere for rejection and later led to self-rejection. You see, Sis, our salvation did not cost us anything, but it cost Jesus everything. Those life-shaping words spoke over me as a child did not cost my parents anything but it eventually cost me my soul.

From the age of 14 to 35, I was in a committed relationship with the man who became my then-husband. This man was seven years my senior and at that time in my life, I believed he was an answer to a never prayed prayer. For only God knows where the path I was on would have led. Yet even this relationship choice would continue to cost me something I didn't have. Sis, I share this phase of the process to show you that even minute moments can have a great cost, and although we are not writing checks for these choices, they are costing us. My early seeding process of others' thoughts and opinions of me cost me my self-esteem. I now understand no one can think higher thoughts of you than you are thinking of yourself. For someone else to value me I had to first discover the value in me. I had to discover myself, and to do this required action on my part. Not just my faith in God, but I had to put some work in, and the results didn't happen overnight.

No, healing is progressive and requires a process. It will require us to work the Word. "Don't just listen to the Word, and so deceive yourself. Do what it says," James 1:22. We have to put into action what the Word of God is saying. We would not water our house plants with contaminated water. We would water them with nourishing water and this is what we have to do for our souls. Our empty glasses need filling and it will require the water of the Word of God for this filling to obtain healing. Empty glasses can be refilled.

As you allow The Healer to come in and replenish your soul, the healing will begin to manifest. You will be able to look over those events and remember the cost but thank God for the lessons learned. You will allow all regret to dissipate as healing flows over those events and life moments that helped to make you the marvelous being you are. Sis healing is the children's bread. JESUS died on the cross and paid the price for your healing. Now let us reach up and out of those circumstances and grab hold of this healing that has been paid for. If we were dining at a fine restaurant and someone decided to pay for our meal, we would politely accept it. Let us accept the gift of healing that has already been paid for on our behalf.

On the cross when JESUS said, "It is finished," He was ultimately saying, "Bill paid in full."

Chapter 12: Learning in Reverse...It Is Not Your Fault

"Now all glory to God, who is able to keep you from falling away and will bring you with great joy into His glorious presence without a single fault." Jude 1:24

Well, Sis, as you can see this book is more than a sultry adulterous relationship or being a side chick. Even though I was in both positions as you may have been also. No, this book is an extended healing hand helping you to gain a clearer perspective of many life events and moments that led us to accept less than we deserved in any given situation. This is not a book to point blame or to impart shame on us nor any of the waterers in our life. In fact, this is a hand of love and rejuvenation.

Helping you to see that woman in the mirror who has often been ignored and neglected. This book is for her. So, Sis, as we continue our journey of healing the other woman, let's stop right here and take a deep breath. Take the palms of your hands and place both over your womb while breathing light deeply into those dark places and breathing out love. As the light shines on those dark hidden areas, let's allow love to saturate those places as they are being revealed and healed.

Let's continue to take a look at the process JESUS went through for us, becoming our living example of what it means to go through the process and as we study this process, we will identify the fruit that is required to get to the harvest of promise. Matt 7:20 says, "You shall know them by their fruit" and what are the fruits: Galatians 5:22. We identified earlier that we must believe. First, Mary had to believe what the angel of God said to her which was the seeding process before she could produce the fruit known as JESUS.

The first fruit we will focus on producing will be ***humility.*** As we consider JESUS' birth. We see Him being placed in the womb of a virgin woman. This means He came in the form of a man to be birthed out of a woman. Now I don't know about you but when I look at this, I remember that God could have placed JESUS here as an adult just like God did with Adam and Eve. Yet instead, God allowed JESUS to be born out of the womb of a woman. This took humility as God placed himself inside of a woman to endure the process of being parented by a woman.

When He is God and submits to no one above Himself. Yet, He humbled himself to go through this process to redeem you and me. Therefore, while we are enduring the process of healing the other woman, we may go through phases that will take us to places that may require us to take a step back in man's eyes and that may be uncomfortable in order to advance God's purpose in our lives on this earth as it is in heaven, and this will require us to be humbled.

As females and males, we are created with natural instincts and desires. Our bodies were created for pleasurable sensations that were given to be activated at a certain time in all of our lives. This predesignated time was "marriage".

However, in many of us, this sensation was ignited much earlier than the designated place of marriage. You see the designated place of marriage was created to be the perfect, uninhibited, safe, and sanctified place for sex. For the Bible tells us that the marriage bed is undefiled. However, for some of us, life happens before we arrive at this place of marriage.

For me, life happened when I was around four years old. I have this vision of being laid on a beanbag. Here, I could see the dining room table to my left, and in front of me, I could see my dollhouse. This view also included a figure standing or leaning over me. Whenever this vision appears, it makes me squeeze my stomach muscles tight and intensely. I'm bracing myself for something. I then began to hold my breath and then it all ended. It makes me sad every time I see it. It makes my heart race and often comes with a feeling of fear and shame. As a result of being sexually stimulated at this age not only did my body develop physically early but also did my desire for sex.

When speaking to JESUS about this vision I often ask Him "Is this me or is it a vision of someone else?" Truthfully it just may be me, but my mind may not be able to handle the truth of this fact. After sitting and talking to a young lady during a yoni steam, I learned it was me. During the event as a child, I stepped outside of myself to protect myself. Separating my spiritual being from my body to protect the innocence within me. Almost like detachment from reality which I would often do during other sexual encounters as I got older, because I knew they were not right for me. As time went on, I have stopped asking, "Is it me?" and started asking, "What would you have me to learn from this vision?"

The answer was, "No, it's not your fault," That no matter who the little girl is in the vision, it is not her fault. This is what I feel led to say to you Sis and anyone who may have encountered someone mishandling your body without your permission. No, it was not your fault. No matter the age. When a child is touched in an inappropriate sexual manner it awakens natural reflexes in that child.

If a female child is stimulated sexually, it awakens their natural sexual desires. So, let's say Sis you're a child and someone starts to rub his hands or mouth sensually on your breast your body may naturally feel pleasure. Even if it's someone doing it without your permission. Someone old enough to know better or even forcefully.

Whatever the situation, the body does not know this should not be happening and that this person is violating you. This is where the head and the body may have conflict and respond to the stimuli differently. All the body knows is that these sensations are natural, and it was created to have a response. Similar to fear. If you are watching a scary movie, the body does not know that this fear is not real, but it is going to react to the fear it is feeling. So, when a child is sexually violated, their body responds accordingly as if this occurrence is bringing pleasure.

The body is not able to identify if what's happening is wrong or right, or is it with or without consent. Its only work is to feel what is being made to feel, and so it does. Being touched gives your body pleasure, and no matter the circumstances, it will be feeling it. Please understand that this reflex is not your fault, and it does not dismiss the fact that you were just violated. Oftentimes when someone is violated, the violator talks or smiles at the child and says things like:

"It feels good, doesn't it... doesn't it?"

"Oh, you like this, don't you...?"

"Relax, so it won't hurt."

"I would never hurt you."

This is called programming. When someone tells you what to say, what you are feeling, or what you have to do to help you understand what you are feeling that process is called programming. They are attempting to change the way you may feel or think about what is happening into how they want you to feel and think about what's happening. But once the stimulation has taken place outside of its predestined destiny of marriage the body will want it.

The body will naturally react to certain situations and circumstances as a response to that stimulation. Many children will start to touch themselves or other children looking for that feeling. We call it being horny and believe it or not being horny is a natural response we should have in the context and boundaries of marriage, but when a child is violated, they now have these desires awakened with no outlet. Resulting in victims becoming violators and or promiscuous until they get healed. So, Sis, I'm not here to justify any behavior or to say this has happened to you. But I am here to state that healing starts with revealing. Revealing our truths to ourselves for GOD already knows.

For JESUS said, "I come to set the captives free..." Let's get free. Let's be real with ourselves so we can also be real with others. For me when discussing an event that was taking place in my family with a male violating a child, I had to confront this area in my memory that was coming forth. It wasn't new to me, but I thought I dealt with it. I started recalling sexual experiences I had prior to losing my virginity. You know all the rubbing and touching. Even allowing oral stimulation to happen to me as a child where I felt like the predator in the end. All of which I carried around shame and regret over.

But, and I say "But" strongly, because then I asked Holy Spirit to come into those memories and into the present moment and reveal all that which was hidden and then to heal me, those who hurt me, and all that was hurting. That's when Holy Spirit showed me that I was like a donut with a hole in the middle, and life was the frosting. But if I invited Holy Spirit to come into this area of my life, He would fill the center. So I did and that's why I am sharing this with you. Sis let's invite Holy Spirit into this area. He is all-knowing, and He holds you and me blameless. For no matter the situation or the circumstances It's Not Your Fault. You are NOT to Blame.

In Christ JESUS be healed.

JESUS is not just the God of destiny, but He is also the God of the detour. He has a plan for you to make your crooked places straight.

Therefore, now there is no condemnation for those who are IN Christ JESUS. (Romans 8:1) So Father "Abba", I gratefully humbly submit every circumstance, choice, and situation before You at Your feet and I repent for not prioritizing me. For not always choosing me even if it hurt. Now Holy Spirit I invite you into these spaces and places in my heart and I thank You for filling these desolated places with Your living water. I thank You for the saturation of Love and Peace. I release the guilt, blame, and shame unto You as they were nailed in Your hand JESUS for me on Calvary. For I receive Your healing light today Yahweh Amen.

Chapter 13: Thirsty

JESUS on the cross said "I thirst." ...John 19:28

After coming from a place of learning it was not my fault. That the things that happened to me do not define who I am nor my destiny. Going through that part in the process of healing the other woman was draining. I would feel thirsty like I needed an infilling for my soul. My soul was thirsty but not for natural water. I needed Holy Spirit to infill me with more of Him in order for me to continue with this process of healing the other woman, and then I remember I wasn't the first one to be thirsty which led me to the Word.

John 19:28 says, "After this, JESUS knowing that all was now finished, said (to fulfill the scripture), 'I thirst.'" Yet when they offered JESUS something to drink prior to this, He turned it down. For it was wine mixed with myrrh (Mark 15;23) which would have numbed Him, and He didn't want to be numb when He finished the process. Instead, He CHOSE to feel the shame, doubt, guilt, unbelief, embarrassment, and abandonment that was consuming me. You name it, He felt it. If you've been through it. He knows what that pain feels like. He chose to feel every emotion and feeling I would ever encounter. However, after He felt all of these things you and I would endure, it left Him thirsty. After we conclude life-changing moments sent to reveal and heal, we also will become thirsty. You see, it is not a sin to be thirsty, but the problem comes from where we choose to be filled. For everything is not for our consumption. We cannot drink from the pain of the past and expect to heal. As the process reveals the pains of our past, we must drink from the water of God's Word and not the temporary things of this world. JESUS was on His way to Samaria (John 4) and stopped at a well to talk to a woman who was "thirsty." While talking to this woman, JESUS revealed to her the truth about her past and her present. He said to her, "...you have had five husbands, and the man you now have is not your husband...." Prior to making this statement to the woman, JESUS said to her, *"If* you knew who was asking you to drink, you would ask him for a drink. And the drink he has you would thirst NO more."

Ok.... pause break.... who can relate? You see you may not have married all the men you have had sex with but let's be real. Let's replace the word in the passage from "husband" to "sexual partner or boyfriend". I don't know about you but JESUS was talking to me here. You see, He said to her, "If you knew who was asking you for a drink, you would have asked Him before He could ask you." He also took the time to reveal to her what and why she had to continue to come to the well for water because her belief system was telling her that the thirst she had could only be fulfilled by having a man or husband. That this thirst could be satisfied by the things of this world.

No, the thirst she had could only be fulfilled by God. He had to take her back to her past in order to help her move forward toward the work He had for her. Also, please note that her past would not define her future. As JESUS said He came to set the captives free not to condemn. Free from the bondage of the way we see ourselves. For it is not our business or concern how others view us but it's how we view ourselves and our past that matters. We have to be willing to drop the negative thoughts of our past in order to grab hold of the Word of God to be set free. John 8:31 "...JESUS said, 'If you hold to my teachings, you are really my disciples. Then you will know the truth, and the truth will set you free.'"

Come on, let's continue to think here. Why is JESUS asking this woman a question? JESUS all-knowing is asking a question. I have learned to pay close attention when God is asking a question. His questions are not for His information as He already knows the answer, but His question is to grab our attention and help us to better see what we have been seeing incorrectly, correctly. This is to bring revelations of the misinterpreted information we have previously received.

Now let's look back at what He asked her. "Will you give Me a drink?" This is the same JESUS who would later turn down a drink and she actually never even gives JESUS any water.

What I like most about this passage is the question this woman asked JESUS, "Where can I get this water you are talking about?" When you are thirsty, any water won't do, Sis.

This woman was at a place in the process of healing the other woman that she now wanted this water JESUS was speaking about. She was willing to say to God, "I thirst." She had been operating from a wounded and bruised place of hurt, anger, fear, disappointment, abandonment, unbelief, shame, guilt, and doubt. These wounds and bruises had caused her to seek refuge or water from men who were just as broken and empty as she was. This woman was so thirsty and tired of coming to this well that her soul was asking the question, not her pride nor ego. I believe her soul was at a place of desperation, and JESUS knew this, and that's why He took the time to wait for her at the well. To fill her glass.

Can you imagine picking up an empty glass putting it to your lips and then getting disappointed when you put it down and are still thirsty? Well, that's what this woman was experiencing, and this is what happens to us every time we enter into a relationship with a man that is unavailable. We pour out what we don't have in hopes this empty man will fill us back up. Nope, not going to happen. We must be willing to allow our souls to be filled by JESUS, and just like this woman, JESUS has been waiting for us to cry out "where can I get this water" for "I thirst". Therefore, Sis, it is my prayer, as you are reading this book, you are taking the time and space to allow Holy Spirit to refill your glass until it overflows unto those dry and desolated places in your life. Until those places reveal a well-nourished and healed garden.

"Now to Him who is able to do exceedingly abundantly above all that we ask or think, according to the power that works in us,"
Ephesians 3:20

Chapter 14: Stop Circling the Parking Lot

"For I know the plans I have for you, declares the Lord, plans to prosper you and not to harm you, plans to give you hope and a future" Jeremiah 29:11

One day, I was on the phone with B. We would be on the phone for endless hours throughout the day while he and my husband were at work. On this day I was working outside of my home, and I then decided to make a bank run. B asked me what bank I was at and just so happened he was about to drive past this location. I suddenly grew afraid and excited as a part of me wanted to see him, but the other part feared he would see me and reject me. I had gained a lot of weight since he last saw me when we were kids. However, I moved past this fear and we decided to meet anyway. As he got into my vehicle, the first words that came out of his mouth were, "Wow, you're beautiful." Now he did not shout these words but mumbled them. Yet they were as clear as a shout and my eyes watered at that moment. Right then I knew I was done.

Why did those words have such an effect on me? Because I was dry. I was thirsty. My then-husband never said things like that to me or made me feel beautiful. Up until that moment I had never really felt beautiful. I may have felt sexy being a certain physical size but not beautiful. Growing up many people would tell me I looked like my mother, and that became a source of the problem for me. Why, because my mother would often make the same comparison, yet she did not believe she was beautiful. So, it became hard to believe I was beautiful when the woman I was being compared to felt she was ugly. So, when B said those words to me on that day, it was as if I heard them and believed them for the first time, and now the problem I was facing was being in my vehicle with a married unavailable man. An unavailable man who was offering me something to drink and me being so desolate that I could not even see he was just as thirsty as me. This was the first encounter with B that led to many more. It was the start of an unfruitful affair.

Tasha Cobbs Leonard has a song titled Fill Me Up that I love. The song is asking God to fill us up until we overflow. As JESUS said, "I come so that you may have life and life overflowing." This is a filled life. Not an empty glass, not a half-filled glass, not even a glass filled to the rim. But this is a glass that is overflowing onto its saucer (quote from Lisa Nichols), and this overflow comes from JESUS and not from a man. The Word of GOD says, "Out of your belly shall flow rivers of living water." This is the living water JESUS was speaking about when He said, "...you would have asked Him, and He would have given you living water." (John4:10)

Stop circling the parking lot, Sis. For there are times in life when we have plans that require us to move out of one state of mind into another. Let's imagine we are headed to a shopping mall during the holiday season. The parking lots are full. We see someone's brake lights on, and we decide in our mind they are about to move out of this space. So, we wait. Sometimes this car may be taking too long so we begin to circle around in hopes of either finding another parking space or that this car will get the hint. After waiting we tell ourselves to be patient. We figure they see us waiting and will hurry up and move out, but we soon notice this doesn't happen. So now we grow a little irritated and hunk our car horn to get their attention. Only for them to say "no I'm not about to come out ... I'm just sitting here." We then get mad and feel like they wasted our time.

We often repeat this cycle many times in life. We get into relationships where we know this person is in an occupied space. Whether the space is occupied with another individual, a career, kids, themselves, or money. Whatever they are consumed with or preoccupied with. The thing that gets most of their time and attention. Which means this space is not available. Thus, this person is not available. We have to stop telling ourselves that if we keep waiting a little longer, they will eventually see us waiting and make a decision to move this process along. For what we fail to realize about this state is that indecisiveness is a decision.

It's just not the decision we were hoping for. Therefore, instead of us circling this full parking lot. Continually repeating this cycle. Lying in bed replaying the same conversations in our head over and over. Daydreaming about this space becoming available. We need to ask the question upfront before we invest the most valuable asset of our time in waiting for this space to become available. Are you available? Married but not happy at the moment does not equal available. Married but separated does not equal available. No, they are occupied spaces. Having a girlfriend but she's selfish and travels a lot does not equal available. Dating multiple women or sexing multiple women does not equal available. Pursuing money and the only time you have for the person of interest is to have sex and sleep does not equal available. At home with your husband but his thoughts are not present with you does not equal available. No, all of these spaces are occupied, and no matter how patient you are, if this person is not ready to move or change, they are not moving or changing. Therefore, we must develop a mindset of making wiser smarter choices sooner rather than later for ourselves. We have to stop circling the parking lot repeating the same thing over again.

Sis, please note an unavailable man is an empty glass. He cannot give you what you need or want because he doesn't have it. He's looking for a well just like you are. However, a problem with being thirsty is not knowing just how thirsty you are which often leads to destruction. I discovered this over the course of the affair with B and the death of my then marriage. As we continue on this journey of healing let's consider our source of fulfillment. Let's remember unavailable equals thirsty and JESUS is our only source of living water. Not a man, woman, child, house, or money can fulfill that dry, desolate, or thirst in our life. We must reach out as the woman did with the issue of blood and we have to ask for the water as the woman did at the well. It is up to you and me to stay hydrated. We must drink from the water of God's Word daily. We cannot get so consumed with the cares of life that we forget that in order to be healthy enough to pour out into others we have to first be overflowing ourselves.

Chapter 15: Pieces of Me

"Men, I can see that our voyage is going to be disastrous and bring great loss to ship and cargo, and to our own lives also." But the centurion, instead of listening to what Paul said, followed the advice of the pilot and of the owner of the ship. Acts 27: 10-11

It was a beautiful day in September when I met my then-husband. It was the first Friday of my 9th-grade year. I was late for school on this particular day as I had to pack for a weekend stay at a friend's house. It was the first week of school so I was not missing anything and besides I was an honor roll student who barely had to study so I knew I could catch up. As I was strolling along to school several cars would stop, with men making attempts to give me their telephone numbers. I would not stop but at the same time, this was flattering to me. When a guy would honk the horn or yell out to get my attention it was a boost to my ego.

It symbolized they thought I was sexy or attractive. That someone wanted me even if it was just for my body. I knew sex was what they wanted, and I was not interested but I liked the attention. Many of the times the guys in the cars were much older than I was so my response would be a simple "you're too old" while I continued to walk. Thinking about it now, many of the guys in the cars could have gotten offended by that statement but most would just ask me my age, and I would proudly reply, "14." Yes, I was 14 years old attracting the attention of many older guys. So, on this day my response to the guy in this car was the same. However, he did not seem fazed by my response. Instead, he put the car in reverse on a busy street while cars were moving at a rapid speed. The passenger window suddenly rolled down and someone reached out a piece of paper with a telephone number on it. I do not recall giving him mine as that fact has always been a mystery.

Later that evening while over at my friend's house we decided to contact some of the guys we had met earlier that day and so I paged the number on the paper. Shortly after the phone rang, the mystery man from the car was on the other end. We talked briefly as my friends, and I now had plans to go out with some other guys. I informed the caller whom I will refer to as "A" that I would call him back later, but I never did.

Several days went by and the weekend was now over, and I was back at home. One evening, I was on the telephone with a guy when there was an alert from the call waiting. I answered and it was A. I was shocked he was calling me at home as I did not recall giving him my phone number. Truthfully, I had no intentions of calling him ever again. Not that he had done anything wrong. I just was not interested. Which later I will find to be a pattern in my life.

At this time, I was interested in someone else and that is where my attention was. When I am interested in someone, I am only interested in them. So, when A called, I told him I would call him back but never did. However, after several days of me telling A I would call him back, he decided to tell me how he felt. He started yelling, "You said you're going to call me the f-word back and you never call me the f-word back."

Now I was shocked but impressed at the same time. I laughed at him and then promised I would call him back this time. So, when I concluded my prior call, I called him back. I thought this guy must really like me based on his reaction to me not calling him back. Again, I was 14 and I thought I knew so much about life. It took me 20 more years to see this was not a healthy response from a healthy person. I was making assumptions about what it meant to truly be interested in someone based on my life experiences at that age. I had never seen a healthy relationship between a man and a woman modeled before me.

I had seen several people in relationships, but none looked like anything I wanted for myself. Many of the relationships I saw involved a man wanting and begging to be with the woman. So, this is what I thought a healthy relationship looked like. When I often liked a guy, it never seemed to work out so I thought maybe I should give this relationship with 'A' a try. I thought it would be easier to like someone who liked me more than I liked him, and this is what I did. I built a 22-year relationship and marriage off of this principle.

You see, I was making do with the limited information I had. It did not have to be right as I did not know it was wrong. I was more focused on having someone to love and someone to love me. This relationship with A validated my worth at the time. Someone was finally showing up consistently for me. My youth was hard, and I was always focused and determined to have a better life than what I saw other women around me having. 'A' for me was what I would now call a safe place. I never had to give all of me to be with A as he was also an empty glass when we met. So, all I had to give him was pieces of me that seemed to satisfy him. As the years continued, he never required or even noticed he did not have all of me. My relationship with A did not require me to truly be the highest expression of myself. In fact, it did not challenge me. It was like the effort I had to put into my grade schoolwork. Not much. I did love A and thought I was giving him all of me, but sometimes the problem with being broken or empty is you may not even know you're broken or empty.

I entered this relationship with A when I was 14 years old and thought I knew what love was. Over the course of our relationship and marriage, I did not realize there was a difference between loving someone and being in love with them. I thought this was inclusive. Therefore, I did not know that entering marriage at 20 when I had not yet learned myself or expressed many of the masked feelings I had would lead to divorce after 15 years.

Before we married, my pastor said to me after our first and only pre-marriage counseling session, "Vonnie, if you marry him, you will always be pulling him along."

I was naïve when he said this to me and I was hearing the pastor through the wounds of my past, and therefore I thought he was saying I was not worthy of someone marrying me. Abandonment and rejection were still present in my life as I had not yet healed. So, I did not ask him for clarification to help me better understand what he meant. No, I leaned to my own understanding and concluded I was worthy, and I was going to prove the pastor wrong. I set in my mind just like the men on the ship with Paul that I was going to get to my destination of being loved no matter what the pastor thought about me, and I concluded the pastor did not know best. I had not yet learned what it meant to submit to the wise counsel of someone with a greater anointing to hear from God for the situation. In fact, I did not really know what it meant to submit to authority as those living in authority over me rarely made decisions I agreed with. I was still living in survival mode as I had been my whole life. Doing what I thought was right I entered into a marriage with A despite the advice of my pastor.

Throughout my life, I often thought people could see my wounds when they looked at me. I thought they could see the daughter of a woman who was suffering from substance abuse. The daughter of a man who did not stick around to tuck her in at night. A little girl who had to use newspaper for toilet tissue. The little girl who had to live in shelters. The girl who was hit by a car and who may not be able to have children. The girl who never felt pretty or smart despite her accomplishments. The young lady who did not feel worthy.

I thought this was why B did not choose me over those other girls. I thought when someone saw me, they saw all these wounds. As a coping mechanism, I would overcompensate for these areas of inadequacy. So, I gave 'A' an ultimatum to marry me because I didn't want people looking at me and thinking I was shacking up with someone I was not married to. So, I pressured A to marry me because I did not want to continue sinning against God and therefore, I thought this was a good reason to get married. But it was not a God reason to marry. In fact, I was marrying because I thought it would show others that despite all those wounds, they could see somebody wanted to love me. When this was not the truth at all. 'A' had not even noticed my wounds for having his own and therefore I believe the pastor made his comment. I did not notice A's wounds until we were married, but even then, because I was used to overcompensating, I would overlook many of them. I would make attempts to help fix his wounds while ignoring my own and this self-neglect would cost me.

Like myself A had many insecurities which would cause him to display rages of jealousy toward me. He did not trust me to be out of his sight. He always thought I would cheat on him if I was not with him. To help him feel secure with our relationship I would do things like calling him to tell him every place I went and every stop I would make. However, if I was at any place longer than he thought I should be there, he would call to voice his concern. For me, I thought this meant he really loved me and was concerned about my well-being.

I thought just like his initial phone call to me when I was 14 years old when he yelled at me, that he really liked me. As time went on this behavior became exhausting because no matter what I did it did not make him feel secure. I even quit my job where I was making most of the household income to follow a dream thinking this would help our relationship, but it didn't either. The calls would be more frequent. One day I was out working and when I came home, he wanted to smell my panties to see if I had been somewhere having sex. These events continued to drain an already empty glass. The longer I stayed in the marriage the more afflictions my soul took. When you are wounded, and your soul is in pieces you are unable to properly receive information given to you. You will misinterpret what is being said because the wound is like a filter on the lens of some eyeglasses. Until you clean those lenses to see properly everything you see will be distorted. This is how it was for me. I had been looking at life through the lens of abandonment, shame, and rejection. I had wounds from my past that caused my soul to be in pieces.

Therefore, when I entered the relationship and marriage to A I was not in a healed state to assess what I was entering. I thought the pieces of me were enough to accomplish my goal of loving and being loved. However, the longer I stayed in the relationship the more fragmented my soul became. Both A and I needed healing, yet we couldn't see it. I thought I could help heal A and then I would get what I needed. But this was not the case. We could only be healed by The Healer, and I had to learn this as time went on and this became dangerous.

Chapter 16: Traveling on Broken Pieces

"Much time had been lost, and sailing had already become dangerous...." Acts 27:10

After the first 10 years of marriage, I started to take notice that something was missing. At this time, I had developed a more seasoned relationship with Christ JESUS and was studying His Word. I had even been ordained as an elder in the church I was attending. I mean life was good so why was there still that feeling of something being missing. I thought the marriage would bring me joy and fulfillment and for the most part, I was happy but not whole.

I was constantly thinking about the future and how obtaining certain things would fulfill me and make me whole. I thought the one thing I had yet to have but wanted was a child. Surely, this would make me whole, but after having my son, I did not have any joy, and guess what, I was not whole either. It was like this addition was not adding but subtracting. Yes, I love my son, yet my soul was still in pieces. Something was still missing, and I had checked all the boxes.

So, what was I to do now? I was lost. I was beyond thirsty. I was dehydrated. I was desperate for a filling. Within four days of giving birth to my son, I was readmitted to the hospital for congestive heart failure. My body was screaming out what my mouth could not find the words to say, "I am not happy, I am not feeling joy, I am overwhelmed, **I am not whole**." I was literally drowning in my own fluids. According to the Cambridge English Dictionary, the meaning of the word congestion is "to overfill, overcrowded, clogged." My soul was at a place where it could not take on another thing until the overload was lifted. I was in an underground tunnel in a traffic jam and I had to find out why I was sitting in this overcrowded, clogged space. I couldn't move forward to get out of this space my soul was in and I couldn't go back either. It took me another three years to gain a clear perspective of what was taking place within my mind and body that my mouth was unable to communicate.

I had started laying before God seeking an understanding of what I was feeling. My body constantly had this yearning feeling. A feeling like when you are about to reach a climax but suddenly the person stops abruptly, and it feels like you're stuck in neutral. This is a weird feeling and until you get the actual relief your body feels angry and crazy. Well, this is how I felt for about three years after giving birth to my son, and I could not find the words to express what I was feeling.

I had prayed to God for over ten years to have a child and to be a mother and now that prayer had been answered but I still wasn't fulfilled. I couldn't communicate this to anyone. Surely, they would think I was ungrateful. I was even afraid to really cry out to God. I felt shame and conviction. I knew God loved me and I often found myself praying 'God, please save me again... please show me...me.' Yes, I wanted God to show me myself and not my husband or anyone else. I wanted to see me as He sees me and how I was at that moment. During this time in my marriage my husband was working late nights so I would often be left with this longing in my body and mind.

I started watching movies at night after my son was in bed. I would eat red velvet cheesecake, lo mein, and drink wine. One particular night after this session my head started hurting really bad. I started to cry out to the Lord to take the pain away and save me to raise my son, but the headache didn't leave. I contacted my pastor who was also my naturopathic doctor the next day and she instructed me to take my blood pressure. The reading was considered high. However, before she recommended treatment, she asked me some probing and personal questions, but I didn't have the answers to those questions. The answers I had were not the answers she expected to hear from me after 14 years of marriage. Many of my responses were surprising to her. She went on to give me a medical protocol to alleviate the headache and to bring down my pressure.

As time went on even this medication didn't work any longer which led me right back to the Source, God. I was now pursuing God for clarity of something the pastor had said to me. She said she had been pursuing God about why many of her patients and church members were suffering from illnesses such as high blood pressure etc. She said God showed her that the people did not want "The Truth", they just wanted relief. You see when I called with the throbbing pain I didn't want "The Truth". No, I wanted her to give me something to relieve the pain. Yet I wasn't even telling her the truth of what I was feeling or doing. If I had told her what I was eating and drinking, I thought she would judge me and make me feel worse than I was already feeling. Unknowingly I had been self-medicating to cope with these uncommunicated feelings just as my mom had done for years was drugs and alcohol. The difference was my drug of choice was now food, but the concept was still the same. I wanted to be numb to my reality instead of telling the truth and receiving "The Truth". This is when B showed up in my life and the affair began. The now-empty glass was breaking from all of the pressure and demands being put upon it.

You see, the container or glass that was housing my soul was empty, yet life was demanding the glass should give it something that was not there. My soul was like a bank account that was no longer receiving deposits but someone was constantly making withdrawals. This is what A had been doing for the 22 years within our relationship. He would come to me to make decisions for our family. The responsibility for the bills and household often fell on my shoulders. Yes, A was a hard worker and that was his main priority. This is what he thought it meant to be a husband as he never saw this role demonstrated healthy before him.

So, he was just going along with the flow as I was. However, this had become draining and suffocating for me. I was a place he could come to drink from but he was not a place I could fill up at. In order for any relationship to be healthy, there has to be an exchange between the parties. Both should be equally giving. Not one more than the other overall. There has to be an equal exchange. This deficit left my soul beyond thirsty, it was dehydrated, and the pressure placed from all of these external forces caused my glass to crack into pieces. I had given a piece of me to A. Another piece to B. The church had a piece of me. Many of the relationships in between had pieces of me and the last piece went to my son. At this point in my life, I had lost my identity. I had become whatever the person in front of me needed me to be. Even though the affair highlighted these issues for me it was also draining from me more than it was giving to me. I had now become so concerned with what B thought of me and what he wanted from me. If he called, I came running.

I was operating from rejection and abandonment. Which ultimately was the spirit of fear. I was afraid if I didn't do what he wanted me to do, then he would replace me just like he did when we were kids. Which stimulated from my dad leaving when I was a kid. Here I was 34 years old and the same boogie man that was in the closet in my youth was still taunting me. I would pray and cry out to God continually for help. I felt like I had yet to be my true authentic self and if I did not make a shift immediately, I was going to die in this state. I felt death was right before me and I had to decide to live as my son deserved his mother to live.

You see I was existing not living. So, I made one of the hardest choices and that was the choice to live at whatever cost. I had to trust that God had me. One day I was washing dishes and I was debating with God about leaving my marriage. I said to God "Lord your word said what You put together let no one tear it apart," and just as clearly I heard Him say "did I put it together." At that moment my life started to flash before my eyes. I saw the vision of me giving A the ultimatum to move in with me, to get married, to sell our previous houses, and to have a child. Then I heard the pastor's voice "you will always be carrying him." I fell to my knees and wept like a baby. I cried for the little girl within me who I had overlooked for so many years. Just like the men who were traveling with Paul, they did not realize that continuing to sail when the winds were blowing would result in the ship being broken into pieces. I, like the men on the boat with Paul, did not submit to the advice given to me not to continue traveling in the state I was in. Instead of taking the advice of the Pastor not to marry A, I continued leaning unto my own understanding.

When I met A I had yet to heal from the trauma caused by B. When I met bet B I had not yet healed from the trauma caused by my parents. I had learned to keep moving despite the traveling conditions. To take a lick and keep on ticking. I did not learn that for a wound to become a scar it has to heal, and healing takes time. Instead, I learned to travel on broken pieces and to force things and situations to happen. I learned to dress up my insecurities with a marriage, houses, cars, a successful career, and now a precious son. Several months after starting the affair with B I made the choice to divorce A. I knew I had to leave to find myself. The true me.

I'm not telling you this to advise you to get a divorce or to condone me having an affair. Sis, I'm just allowing you behind the curtains to some of the decisions I have made in my life. Allowing you to see that little reasons add up to major life decisions, and how one decision affects others. That when we are not healed, we have the potential to infect others on our path. I do not blame anyone for any of the choices I have made throughout life. I have learned to take responsibility for myself and my choices. I now realize somethings had to happen for God to redeem the promises that had not manifested in my bloodline prior to my conception. Due to the things that had taken place within my family line prior to my birth. Remember in the beginning I shared with you what the numbers and order of my birth represent in Hebrew new beginnings and open doors. However, before the doors will be opened some doors had to be closed.

For God in me, is completing some things and birthing some new beginnings through me on this earth as it is in heaven. But to have the new I had to first experience those hard and uncomfortable places in my life. I had to deal with the insecurities, abandonment, and rejection issues from my youth. As these things were still present within me and had an effect on my life, I realized, like Paul, I did not have to go down in this storm.

That even though the winds were raging and roaring that if Jesus said I was going to the other side, and He was on the boat with me. Then no matter what I was facing or what I had done. I was going to make it to the other side. I learned this storm would not take me out and whatever storm you are in or have been through, Sis it will not take you out either. God is the strength you need. For we are His beloved.

Remember when God said to the pastor, "They don't want The Truth." Jesus said in John 14:6, "...I am the Truth..." So what God was saying to the pastor was the people don't want "Me". To gain clarity and healing for our life we have to welcome The Truth into every area of our lives. We have to allow Him to come in and shine His light on those people, places, and dark spaces in our lives that have led us to this place of unfulfillment. This place that is looking for people and relationships to make us happy. To love the areas we are neglecting. I was neglecting myself by being busy with being a wife, mother, elder, professional woman, etc. I was busy at being busy and I forgot the most important part of me. The Woman.

Chapter 17: Open Wounds

"When I was a child, I spoke as a child, I understood as a child, I thought as a child; but when I became a man, I put away childish things." 1 Corinthians 13:11

Another lesson I learned with this experience was the same wounds I had in my youth were exposing themselves because I had not yet dealt with them, but I was praying and asking God to reveal those hidden things that were in me. I was asking God to show me why I was making the choices I was making. It was during this time God revealed I was at a new level in my life. I was no longer the little girl, but I was handling problems and life issues just as I did when I was a little girl.

In my youth, I faced the giant as David did with Goliath the Philistine in 1 Samuel 17, but also like David I dealt with the fruit and not the root of the problem. Therefore, in 2 Samuel 21:15, it says, "Once again there was a battle between the Philistines and Israel..." Meaning, David had to once again come face to face in his manhood with that which he dealt with as a boy. For me, the Philistine was the lie that was continuously telling me I was not enough and that I was weak for allowing B to come back into my life. That I would never be loved. When the true fact is I was not weak at all. This lie also wanted me to believe that because I had lost B to another woman, I needed to take him from another woman to be whole and to prove to myself and others that I was enough. The truth is, I was already enough and loved by God. I just hadn't discovered and embraced self-love yet.

As we continue to read the scripture in 2 Samuel 21:15, it tells us a key clue about David's mental condition at the time of this battle. The scripture says, "David went down with his men to fight against the Philistines (lies and bondage), and he became exhausted." David did not start out exhausted he became exhausted. I like David had also been fighting these same Philistines since my youth, and after 15 years of marriage and 22 years of being in a relationship with A, my soul was exhausted.

I had been constantly fighting these Philistines in my head that was wearing my soul out. My mind was not weak, but it was weary. My physical body was trying to alert me after the birth of my son that it had been running on empty for too long, and just like a car with no gas I was operating on fumes. The problem with continuing in this manner is that eventually, the engine will give out. I have learned that it is when we are running on empty and have nothing else to give then and only then will we actually surrender our all to God and allow him to reveal in order to heal those hidden areas in our lives.

This place of surrender for me was not an overnight thing believe me. I fought God in the beginning and middle. But Sis, I am no match for God. Yet He allowed me to stay in this state of partial surrender as long as I wanted to be there. I must say this was a very uncomfortable place to be. When you are in this state it's like your mind is literally playing tricks on you. I believe if I had gone to a doctor, they may have diagnosed me with bipolar disorder. Bless God I did not and I am not saying do not go see a doctor if you are not feeling well.

For me, as I continued to cry out to God The Great Physician, Holy Spirit reminded me that Deuteronomy 31:6 says, "I the Lord your God will neither leave you nor forsake (forget, emotionally withdraw) from you." It was at that moment I decided to believe God's Word to be true. God showed me His Word was true as he has never left me nor forsaken me during this process of healing the other woman. As I continued to seek Him. He showed me I was not bipolar but stubborn. That I wanted to do what He wanted me to do but I wanted to do it my way and I wanted to know how it was going to work out.

That I wanted to be in control. The problem with this is God will get His way. As He is Alpha. In Genesis 32:24 we see Jacob wrestling with an angel of God and did not want to let go even when the angel instructed him to. What are some of the things God is asking you to let go of Sis? For me, He was asking me to let go of what I had in mind; my need to be perceived as perfect or having it all together. I wanted to be used by God and healed by God, but I did not want to be uncomfortable for God.

I wanted Him to do all these things, but I did not want to let go of the baggage I was carrying to grab hold of His teachings. To know The Truth so I could be set free indeed. Allowing God to place in my hands the fulfillment my soul desired. During this healing phase, God led me to seek counseling which began an enlightening part of the healing journey. Counseling for me was like going to my primary care physician for an annual physical but a physical for my thoughts. I had both spiritual and non-spiritual counselors who all helped me to unpeel the onion surrounding my thoughts.

They helped me to understand that everything I had been through in my life and everything that was still to come was necessary for my mental growth. For maturity. I had to learn that without the storms and the rains, life on this earth would cease to be. That it was not so much about what happened to me or why it had to happen to me, yet more about what each lesson came to teach me. It was like I was in a theatre watching a play called my life. Originally, I was in the nosebleed seat, and how I saw my life was on a screen called victimville. I could see what was happening on the stage but my perspective of the details of what was taking place in my life was not clear.

It was not until I was no longer afraid to ask and answer those uncomfortable and sometimes embarrassing questions to God and the counselors that my seat in the theatre of my life changed. When I gave up the seat as the driver in my life and allowed God to be not only in the driver's seat but the actual driver, then and only then was I able to better see with understanding the events that had taken place in my life. I was able to understand that when you are weary you do not need to go out to battle, David. That some battles are not for me to fight.

I also had to learn that being weary did not mean I was weak. When JESUS was traveling through Samaria in John 4:6, it tells us that JESUS was wearied of His journey, and He then sat down on the well. I believe this was to show us that even the Son of Man grew tired in the process yet He did not give up. He still had to continue on and in Him, we too can continue. But continuing is going to require us to shed the weight of what we had in mind, how we viewed ourselves, and the grip we had on what we thought life would be. Just like the Samaritan woman at the well who had a perspective on where to draw water we too must shift in our thinking allowing Holy Spirit to guide and transform our minds. It's in the transformation of our thinking where healing is released and received. So ultimately, healing starts with forgiveness. One of the hardest things we will face is the process is forgiving ourselves. Yes, us. Why? Because we have a critical role in every relationship we get into and that role is demonstrating how to treat us with love and respect.

Yes, it is our responsibility to show and teach others how to handle us, by how we handle ourselves. If we don't prioritize us, we teach others how not to prioritize us. If we don't choose us, then we teach others how not to choose us. If we are not consistent and committed to us, then others won't be either. Sis, counseling was one of the tools God gave me that helped me to better understand me. I could have rejected the idea of counseling like so many do thinking it would be a waste of my time and money, or that my relationship with God exempted me from needing counseling.

When in fact the Bible speaks of seeking wise counsel. Each of the counselors I have had and still have, helped me to gain a deeper insight into my thought patterns and perspectives. I have learned that life is more than black or white, but in between the black and white is a gray area, and in this area is where I had to learn to shift my thoughts. In this area, I had to learn to be grateful for everything God had brought me through and was taking me to. Sis, as you continue to allow God to reveal in order to heal you may be led to counseling also. It is my prayer for you that whatever instructions God gives to you that you follow them. When JESUS first appeared after His crucifixion, he said to Mary, "Don't touch me I have not yet ascended to my Father." For even JESUS had to go to the Father for His healing because it was all of our sins, shortcomings, insecurities, fears, hurts, and wounds that were upon Him, and these things could only be healed by The Father. Therefore, we must do the same. We must take the fears that have wounded us to The Healer. Later JESUS allowed Thomas to touch Him. Why? Because JESUS wound was now a scar, He could allow Thomas to touch the area that was wounded and not cause him to be reinfected with the infectious thought patterns of the past.

Once we have been healed, we can allow others to touch us without infecting them too. But if we enter into relationships before we are healed, we will hurt others in those areas we have been hurt in. For me, counseling helped me with this process. It allowed me to be vulnerable without being judged. The counselors provided me with tools and skills to help me not to blame myself for things that happened to me. This process taught me how to look at many of my life events from a different perspective. I learned we often "do what we do until we are done with what we did". I say this to say do not rush the healing process. Healing takes time. Be patient with the process and utilize all of the tools God provides.

Chapter 18: Clear Picture

"The rest were to get there on planks or on other pieces of the ship."
Acts 27:44

"You do not have to go down in this," is what I kept telling myself after I filed for divorce and as I was attempting to end the affair with B. During this time, I decided to truly allow God to work on my mind as I realized it was my thoughts of me and my BS (belief systems) that were hindering me. These negative thought patterns were holding me captive from who I knew I was called to be. I still did not have a clear picture of how things would work out, but I knew in my heart there was still more to life than that which I had experienced.

I decided during this time to grab hold of all of the pieces of me that made me who I was and travel on. I learned that in order for an eaglet to learn to fly it would have to be dropped by the eagle. That the drop was not to hurt or harm the eaglet but to help mature the eaglet. For the eaglet was not made to live in the nest its entire life. No, the nest was a temporary place in the process, and for me, all of the life events including the affair were just temporary events in my life and it no longer had to define me if I didn't want it to.

Therefore, like Paul, for me to get to where God had promised to take me, I had to grab ahold of the pieces and allow those pieces to be enough for where I was. These pieces did not represent a complete picture of who I would be or who I was becoming, but I had to travel on the pieces I had left. As I continued to allow God to develop me in this stage of the process, I started to share more of my story with others, and I noticed the more I did, the lighter the burden felt. The shame started to leave. I no longer felt guilty about my choices. For in Jeremiah 1:5, God says, "Before I formed you in the womb, I knew you...." Therefore, the more I trusted in what God said about me, the better I felt about myself. I understood that God knew me before I was ever conceived in my mother's womb. So that meant for me to learn who I was I would have to go to the one who formed me, God. When we want to know how something works, we look to the manufacturer for the instructions and directions. This is what we must also do with our lives. In going to God, I had to make a decision to stop circling the parking lot and discontinue the cycle of allowing myself to be in unavailable relationships. I started changing the way I thought and felt about me. I started loving me. I started choosing me. I started showing up early and leaving late for me. I started to be a professional for me. You see all of the things I was for others, I started being for me.

I started living for me each and every day. I was no longer waiting for someone to move out of the parking space for me. I started creating spaces for me by no longer waiting on other people's occupied spaces. I realized the moment I changed my perspective and belief system about myself, God's favor started custom-making VIP spaces and passes with my name on them. Access was being granted to me. Healing was available to me and I decided to let go of my grip of yesterday and grab ahold of my todays. All the while I was discovering me.

Chapter 19: Beauty Marks

"They made the bronze basin and its bronze stand from the mirrors of the women who served at the entrance to the tent of meeting."
Exodus 38:8

As I continued to allow the process to have its perspective time to work out of me those negative thought patterns and belief systems. I started to see in the eyes of other women the same hurt and woundedness I had. That this journey was bigger than me. That the afflictions were good for me because they led me to you, Sis, and I am not burdened any longer with the weight of these afflictions. I now look at every scar that was once a wound and I smile. As the scars are now my beauty marks.

When God was giving Moses the instructions for making the Tabernacle or Tent of Meetings, He gave specific instructions on the layout and how things would be made within the Tent. One of the places in the Tent was called the Laver. This was the basin made from the looking mirrors of the women who served at the entrance to the Tent. The scriptures say, the women gave up their mirrors for the laver to be built.

This laver was the place you would wash yourself after making a "bloody" sacrifice to God. In this laver, you could see an image of yourself as you washed away the blood that was shed. When the women gave up their mirrors, they were giving up the way they previously saw themselves in order to be willing to see themselves as God sees them. These women had to allow their image to be transformed with the washing away of the past as they looked at the new image reflecting before them in the Laver. These women gave God their mirrors to be beaten down for transformation for the basin to occur. When Adam and Eve ate the apple it was known as the fall, and with this fall we lost our image. We lost the way we saw ourselves. God said let us make man in our own image. Therefore prior to eating the apple, we were seen in the image of God and our mirror reflected an image of God.

Yet, because of the fall sometimes our self-image gets distorted with the things we have been through. When Jesus placed mud on the blind man's eyes, He told him to go wash in the pool. ".. After saying this, he spit on the ground, made some mud with the saliva, and put it on the man's eyes. Go," he told him, "Wash in the Pool of Siloam" (this word means "Sent"). So the man went and washed, and came home seeing. John 9:6-7

The man had to wash away the way he previously saw himself in order to see correctly as his image was distorted. We see this again in Mark 8:24-25 when Jesus spit on the man's eyes and touched the man's eyes the Bible says "He took the blind man by the hand and led him outside the village. When he had spit on the man's eyes and put his hands on him, Jesus asked, "Do you see anything?" He looked up and said, "I see people; they look like trees walking around." Once more, Jesus put his hands on the man's eyes. Then his eyes were opened, his sight was restored, and he saw everything clearly. The first touch was the forgiveness of our sins but the second touch was the washing away of the stain or residue of the things we went through such as the shame and guilt. When we allow the Word to wash us clean from the pain of the past. The past will be like the Egyptian army who perused the Israelites but was overtaken by the Red Sea. The Red Sea washed away the residue of their past and the scripture says, "The enemies you see today, you will see no more."

When we give God our image and He melts it down just like He did when the women gave their mirrors for the laver in the tabernacle. He will melt down the way we perceive ourselves and fill the laver with water so we can wash in it. As we wash in the Word, we will see ourselves not as trees but clearly in the image God sees us. Not broken or bruised but Healed and whole. For I am who God says I am.

As I washed in the laver, I discovered that the scars were no longer scars, but they were beauty marks. I no longer felt shame or blame but I was proud to be a child of God and I now welcomed these beauty marks.

I thank God for bringing me through and I am looking forward to meeting the healed version of you as you allow the healing process to take place in your life. I thank God that each situation that came to break me was used to take me into the predestined purpose for my life. Both of these life events made me cry out ever the more to God. They exposed the fears that were camouflaged as faith. I had to realize my security was not in the boat. For God never said he would save the boat (the relationships or the marriage). No, He promised to save me and that I would get to the place He was calling me to.

Giving God my mirror was like throwing some things overboard. Like anything I was using as a security blanket would ultimately be destroyed on this voyage. This required me to throw overboard some relationships, my pride, the good girl image, and the walls I built for myself, blocking everything with the strong woman mentality of "I do not need anyone." The affair showed me things about myself I would have never guessed were there. It was like a flashlight that was used to shine on those dark corners that were in my life.

The divorce forced me to face the insecurities that were shackling me to others. Yes, it all had to go for me to arrive at this space and place of being healed. Sis, I must say this place feels so good. It is freeing. This is a place I pray you will arrive at too. I believe as you continue your journey of allowing God to reveal in order to heal you to will arrive at this freeing place. There will be some things you will have to throw overboard as well to lighten the load, and a mirror of your image in exchange for the image God has for you.

Sis, you have made tremendous success in your life and in this process of healing the other woman. It is my prayer you will continue to allow God to complete the work He has started in your life as this is just a part of the process. As you will notice we never finished the wine-making process as this part of the journey was just intended to help you endure the beating, pressing, and shaking part of the process. As you begin the fermenting process of isolation know that I am still here. Holding your hand during the process. For you are never alone on this journey of "Healing the Other Woman".

Conclusion

So, healing could be seen as a heart posture. It is something you have to receive and in order to receive it, you have to have an open forgiving heart. Your heart has to be in a place where it can hear from God. When JESUS was hanging in the cross He said, "Father forgive them as they know not what they do." This forgiveness was not just for those who had persecuted Him. It was for those who hurt us, for those we have hurt, and for us. It was for the victim and the victimizer.

It was for you and me. When JESUS was teaching us to pray, He said, "And forgive us our debts (shortcomings, wrongs) as we forgive our debtors (those who have wronged us)." As we forgive others, we are then forgiven, and this is something we must consciously do every day and on purpose. Knowing the forgiveness is for us. It's a part of our healing. Knowing that we too have wronged and hurt others including ourselves creates awareness in us that if JESUS can forgive us then we can receive it and forgive us too.

Within many of us there's an "other woman". The one we allowed to be mistreated. The one we allowed to be neglected and in order to be fulfilled and whole we have to first allow her to be healed. Healing is inside out. It takes place within us. No one can do it for us or give us permission this is something we have to do. We have to be willing to expose our truth and our lies. Be willing to be vulnerable to ourselves and stop judging and condemning us. YES, we did it. Scream it... "HELL YEAH, I Did It." Whatever the "it" was, you did it. But it's what you did not what you do. Past vs Present. So, you cheated it doesn't make you a cheater. We must stop defining who we are by life's circumstances. Yes, you got a divorce, but you are not divorced. We must stop allowing words used out of context as labels to define the divine in us. GOD said to Jacob your name is Israel. GOD said to Adam, "Who told you, you were naked." So, stop it with the labels, guilt, and shame. Forgive you. No, you're not perfect and yes you messed up but guess what everyone has on this earth except JESUS, and He came for our mistakes (mis and take). Therefore, get up and let's do this thing called life on purpose as a healed, fulfilled, and whole woman.

Remember forgiveness will also create a space for us to be vulnerable with ourselves and others. Being vulnerable does not mean we are weak. It is actually a sign of inner strength. For Revelations 12:11 tells us, "And they overcame *and* conquered him because of the blood of the Lamb and because of the word of their testimony..." The blood of the Lamb is the blood Jesus shed on the cross and the word of their testimony is when we are vulnerable enough to share what we have been through so someone else can be healed.

A testimony is when we have completed a test and can now share with someone what we have learned. Not from a place of being wounded but when you can look at the scar and still forgive. Knowing that you are stronger because of your beauty marks. Realizing that your worth and value are not defined by what you went through but by the choice you made to keep going in spite of those afflictions. That we are no longer thirsty for the affirmations of this world, but we are quenched by the Word of God. Sis, we are no longer circling the parking lots waiting on unavailable spaces. No, we have allowed God to mend our broken pieces while we've learned in reverse many of life lessons to gain understanding and not judgment.

Sis, I am so proud of you for partaking in this journey. I thank God, He brought us together for such a time as this. Greater is coming. For your latter days shall be greater than your past. I pray you will continue to surround yourself with wise counsel as you allow God to reveal in order to Heal the Other Woman within.

With Love,

Your Sister on this Journey with You

V

Made in the USA
Monee, IL
14 May 2022

96363686R00066